Leadership for the Schoolhouse

Leadership for the Schoolhouse

How Is It Different?
Why Is It Important?

Thomas J. Sergiovanni

JOSSEY-BASS
A Wiley Company
San Francisco

FIRST PAPERBACK EDITION PUBLISHED IN 2000.

Printed in the United States of America.

Library of Congress Cataloging-in-Publication Data

Sergiovanni, Thomas J.
    Leadership for the schoolhouse: how is it different?: why is it important?/ Thomas Sergiovanni.—1st ed.
        p. cm.—(The Jossey-Bass education series)
    Includes bibliographical references and index.
    ISBN 0-7879-0119-9 (cloth)
    ISBN 0-7879-5542-6 (paper)
    1. Educational leadership—United States. 2. School management and organization—United States. I. Title. II. Series.
    LB2805.S523 1996
    371.2'00973—dc20   95-9405

HB Printing   10 9 8 7 6
PB Printing   10 9 8 7 6 5 4 3 2 1

The Jossey-Bass Education Series

Contents

Preface

Are schools special places? Or are they just organizations that share most of the features and characteristics of all other organizations? I often ask teachers and administrators those questions. They begin by pointing out how schools are similar to other organizations. But as our conversation continues, their list of how schools are different begins to grow. Pretty soon, most conclude that schools are indeed special places.

Let me give you an example. I recently asked a group of teachers and administrators in Kansas City to name familiar enterprises in their community. The Kansas City Royals, Hallmark Cards, Southwestern Bell Telephone Company, General Motors, the local mass transit authority, two banks, a hospital, several churches, a synagogue, a local department store, two other businesses, the Polish-American Mutual Aid Society, the YMCA, a volunteer women's group, a neighborhood association, a civic group, several social clubs, and even the family were mentioned. I then asked each person, representing an enterprise that they had selected, to get into a line by standing next to two others who represented similar enterprises. After some reshuffling, they were arranged in a predictable order. Toward the left end of the line were such organizations as Hallmark Cards, General Motors, the bank, and so on. Then a large gap appeared in the line. To the right side of this gap were the church, social clubs, the volunteer group, the mutual aid association, the family, and other social enterprises. At the far left was General Motors and at the far right was the family.

We stood in that line for some time talking about the principles of leadership that make the organizations to the left of the gap in the line work effectively. But when we tried to apply these same principles to the enterprises to the right of the gap, they didn't seem to fit very well. It was hard to put a finger on the precise leadership principles that guide the enterprises to the right, but it was clear that they were different.

What we did, I think, was to discover a basic principle of leadership. The theories of management, organization, motivation, and control that make sense for some kinds of collectivities do not make sense for others. Good leadership for corporations and other organizations, it appears, may not be good leadership for churches, neighborhood associations, families, and other social enterprises.

The key question is, "Where should schools be placed on this continuum?" Without hesitation, everyone in the Kansas City group agreed that schools belong somewhere on the right side of that gap in the line. Most parents, teachers, policy makers, and ordinary citizens, I believe, agree with them.

Schools should be treated as special cases because they serve as transitional places for children. They stand between the subjective and protected environment of the family, and the objective and exposed environment of the outside world. Relationships between educators and students are characterized as being *in loco parentis*. As this role is played out, teachers and administrators are brought together into a collective practice that resembles a shared stewardship. Schools are responsible for more than developing basic competence in students and passing on the culture of their society. They are also responsible for teaching habits of the mind and habits of the heart. Everything that happens in the schoolhouse has moral overtones that are virtually unmatched by other institutions in our society.

Ideally, the *in loco parentis* role of teachers and administrators is not distant from actual parental roles, but nested within them. Students are best served when teachers, administrators, and parents act in concert—when their complementary roles represent not just a partnership, but a mutually beneficial compact on behalf of students. Within this web of moral commitments and morally held reciprocal responsibilities, schools are best thought of as a kind of moral learning community that enjoys a place within our society very close to the family as a moral nurturing community. Both share affinities with churches that function as spiritual communities; youth clubs that function as friendship communities; and neighborhood associations that function as civic communities.

In practice, however, the differences between schools and other enterprises have not been allowed to count. We now import our theories of leadership from management disciplines anchored in our business schools, and we import our leadership practices from corporations, baseball teams, armies, transportation systems, and other organizations. Imported theories and practices are accompanied by assumptions and beliefs that provide models for how schools should be organized, how schedules should be arranged, how curriculums should be developed and implemented, how teaching and learning should be understood, how students should be assessed, and how teachers should be supervised and evaluated.

A basic theme of this book is that these imports do not serve our real goals. We need to develop our own theories and practices—theories and practices that emerge from and are central to what schools are like, what schools are trying to do, and what kinds of people schools serve. This theme is important for both practical and moral reasons. Practically speaking, imported theories of leadership and the school practices that they promote are not working very well. Criticizing our theories is not the same as criticizing the people who are stuck with them. Most school leaders care, and try to do what is best for students. They are, however, under enormous pressure to change things for the better. In true North American fashion these changes are expected to be implemented quickly. This quick-fix pressure leads many school leaders to look for easy answers that do not result in meaningful change.

To complicate matters, school leaders are exposed to a literature in educational administration that is largely characterless. Most of the theories and ideas quoted in this literature are borrowed from other fields. Translations of this literature for use in staff development often take the form of "pop" management comprised of some new ideas and repackaged old ideas that are offered as simple solutions to difficult problems.

Many school leaders, for example, look to the corporate quality movement for answers. Others link their fate to performance outcomes, site-based management, or corporate versions of "visionary" leadership. Most worry about how to motivate teachers to perform better, and how to monitor and assess this performance in ways that enhance morale and improve productivity. They learn how to use various leadership styles and motivational techniques that are matched to the situations they face. And they learn how to adopt the latest training technology that will allow for the trickling down to the classroom of desired practices that will reform the system. Sometimes they put all these answers together by introducing something called the strategic planning process. But all of these practices are bought or borrowed from places other than the schoolhouse, and very few of these practices have resulted in long-term solutions to our problems.

Why aren't these borrowed practices creating the promised miracles? Could it be that the law of proximity is at play? I think so. The law of proximity states: *The more often we import ideas from afar, the less likely that over time they will make a difference.* The law of proximity works in concert with the law of conservation of information. This law states: *No matter how refined a model becomes, or no matter how effectively a model is translated into practice, it cannot enlarge the basic premises upon which it rests.* The thesis of this book can be summarized by the law of effect, which states: *It is not likely that much progress will be made over time in improving schools unless we accept the reality that leadership for the schoolhouse should be different, and unless we begin to invent our own practice.*

Overview

In this book, I examine existing theories of leadership and provide examples of how their translation into school practice does not serve administrators, teachers, parents, or schools very well. I then provide a framework of ideas, together with examples, that can be used to help create a unique leadership for the schoolhouse—a leadership whose resulting school practices are more community-like, more consistent with the democratic principles of civic virtue advocated by the American founders, more responsive to what we know about human nature, and more responsive to what we know about how students learn and develop.

Chapter One examines the theories of leadership and the school practices that are taken for granted in school operation today. Among them are the familiar Pyramid Theory and Railroad

Theory, and the now-popular High Performance Theory. All three theories originate in the corporate world. The chapter proposes that schools would be better off if they relied less on the corporate models, and more on the democratic legacy promulgated by the American founders and embodied in such sacred documents as the Declaration of Independence, the Constitution, and the Bill of Rights. Following the teachings of Aristotle and Plato, the American founders envisioned a nation bound together by a set of values and a common creed that would define the citizenry as a moral community.

Chapter Two addresses the question "What kind of theory for the schoolhouse?" It argues that theory is important because once accepted, even implicitly, a theory functions as a mindscape that creates the realities we use to make decisions about schooling. Readers are invited to examine a set of standards for theory building as a way to reflect on their own ideas about what is needed. These standards hold that a theory for the schoolhouse needs to be aesthetically pleasing. Its language and images should be beautiful, and it should evoke thoughts that are consistent with the school's human purposes and conditions. A theory for the schoolhouse should be idea based, and should emphasize moral connections. It should evoke sacred images of what goes on, and should compel people to respond for internal rather than external reasons. A theory for the schoolhouse should be responsive to the nature of human rationality. It should acknowledge that humans are motivated in part by self-interest, but have the capacity and the desire to respond in ways that transcend self-interest for higher ideals. A theory for the schoolhouse should provide for decisions about school organization, curriculum, and classroom life that reflect constructivist teaching and learning principles. A theory for the schoolhouse should strive to transform the school in such a way that it becomes a center of inquiry—a place where professional knowledge is created in use as teachers learn together, solve problems together, and inquire together. A theory for the schoolhouse should encourage principals, teachers, parents, and students to be self-managing, to accept responsibility for what they do, and to feel a sense of obligation and commitment to do the right thing.

Chapter Three points out that developing a practice of leadership for the schoolhouse will require a change in the theory of school itself. The change proposed is to understand schools as moral communities. The chapter goes on to provide a framework for understanding community and for building community in schools.

Chapter Four examines how schools as communities can speak to teachers, administrators, parents, and students in a powerful moral voice that compels them to do the right thing. Once this voice is established, it can function as a substitute for the usual management systems and leadership strategies now used to provide direction, and to control people and events. The moral voice of community is anchored in shared values, ideas, and purposes. Several school examples are then provided to illustrate how such agreements are forged. The chapter then concludes with an examination of evidence that demonstrates the link between the establishment of moral voice and the provision of more effective schooling for students.

Instead of continuing to import corporate views of leadership to schools, we should return to our roots. This is the theme of Chapter Five. The roots of school leadership are not found in providing "visionary leadership" as described by corporate writers, but in serving the common good, in ministering to the needs of the school, and in providing the oversight that protects the school and keeps it on a true course, clarifying purposes, promoting unity, and helping people to understand the problems they face and to find solutions. The image proposed for schools is leadership as pedagogy. When leadership as pedagogy is practiced, principals, for example, exercise their stewardship responsibilities by committing themselves to building, serving, caring for, and protecting the school and its purposes. Leadership as pedagogy calls both leader and followers alike to higher levels of commitment, to higher levels of goodness, to higher levels of effort, and to higher levels of accountability.

Chapter Six examines the issue of size. Imported theories of leadership encourage the creation of large schools, the proliferation of administrative goals, the fragmentation of effort, the impersonalization of relationships, and the encouragement of faculty and student subcultures that insulate their members from the broader school culture. The evidence on behalf of small schools reveals that students learn more, discipline problems are fewer, leadership roles increase, and teachers are more collegial and feel more efficacious. Further, and contrary to popular belief, small schools are more cost effective than large ones. Chapter Six also examines the wrenching paradox of continuing to proliferate large schools in the face of compelling evidence that small schools are more effective. It provides suggestions for transforming large schools into smaller school communities.

Few would disagree with the admonition that form should follow function. School decisions should be based on what we believe is good and on what we know is effective for enhancing student academic, social, and moral development. But, too often, imported theories of schooling provide ready-made forms for organization, curriculum development, and teaching and learning. Our job is then to figure out how to craft school goals and develop schooling strategies that fit. Function winds up following form. Chapter Seven addresses this problem, providing a set of standards for decision making based on what research and informed opinion tells us is best for student learning and student development.

Chapter Eight proposes that teacher development is the single most important key to improving schools over the long haul. It argues that the constructivist principles of teaching and learning, which provide a scientific basis for making decisions about what is best for students, should be applied to decisions about what is best for the development of teachers as well. The answer to the question of teacher development will be found in changing school cultures in such a way that schools become learning and inquiring communities for teachers as well as students. The school itself, Chapter Eight argues, must become a center of inquiry.

Chapter Nine examines our present theories of change, and proposes an alternative. Theories of change should reflect the realities within which schools operate. With few exceptions, most of what is now thought to be the case about change is based on assumptions about the real world that don't hold up very well. For example, people assume that schools are managerially tight and culturally loose, but in reality the inverse is more often true. Systematic and detailed planning is accepted as an unquestioned principle, but in reality it backfires more often than it helps. The provision of incentives and disincentives is advocated to push changes along, when in fact it gets in the way of the change adoption process. Imported theories of change are rules based. But life in schools is norms based. Chapter Nine suggests that the solution to the change problem may require the deinstitutionalization of change by cultivating professional communities of teachers who are committed to helping each other and committed to doing their best for children. It provides suggestions for how to reach this goal.

In Chapter Ten, the politics of division that dominates the school decision-making process is examined, and a new politics—the politics of virtue—is proposed as an alternative. The politics of division emerges from a view of human nature that emphasizes self-interest and encourages leadership practice based on contracts and deals, winning and losing. The politics of virtue, by contrast, is motivated by a shared commitment to the common good, and is guided by protections that ensure the rights and responsibilities of individuals. The politics of virtue depends heavily on the cultivation of civic virtue expressed as a willingness of principals, parents, and teachers to subordinate their own private interests for the general good of the school. A case is also made for cultivating civic virtue among students as a way to increase their commitment to school goals and purposes, and to facilitate character development.

Two issues keep reappearing throughout the book. Both are examined in the Postscript. One is the issue of absolute versus relative merit. The theories that are used to run corporations, for example, are not good or bad in an absolute sense any more than the theories that should be used to run schools are good or bad in an absolute sense. Corporate theories of leadership are good for corporations and similar enterprises, but bad for schools and similar enterprises. And the inverse is also true. The second issue involves the question of finding a balance between values of individualism and community. The politically correct solution is to cut the deck in half by giving each equal attention. The position of this book, however, is that—given present conditions—we need a correction that favors community. Over the short term, at least, we need theories of schooling and theories of school leadership that give more attention to bringing people together, that give more attention to how we are alike than to how we are different, and that give more attention to the cultivation of civic virtue than to the development of individual and idiosyncratic definitions of morality.

Where Do We Go Next?

Calling for a change in our theories and a change in our practices raises the chicken-and-egg problem. Present theories of schooling confirm themselves by encouraging the adoption of complementary practices. School size is a good example. In order for present theories to work, we need large schools that allow for a considerable amount of role differentiation. The theories presuppose the allocation of responsibilities by hierarchy, the fragmentation of the curriculum, the imposition of lots of impersonal rules and regulations, and the employment of many assistant principals and other specialists. Once these features are in place, they reinforce our need for large schools. Large schools need these features to operate, and the cycle continues.

Just how do we break out of this epistemological trap? I wish I knew for sure. I do know, however, that before we can find the answer, we need first to acknowledge that we have a problem, and then we need to understand that problem. And finally, we need to have a look at some possible alternatives that will encourage us to think differently. Once we are committed to change, and once we kindle the right kind of discussion among teachers, administrators, and parents, I think a number of worthy answers will appear in schools across the continent.

My intent in writing this book was to help inspire the necessary commitment, and to help facilitate the needed discussion. It was Karl Popper who noted that theories should be offered in an invitational mode. Good theories don't get everything right, but elicit the kind of criticism and thoughtful reflection that leads to better ways of looking at things, and that leads to closer approximations of reality. I think we have the problem nailed down pretty firmly. The theories of leadership we now have do not work very well in schools. I hope this book will help us to figure out ways to get this problem resolved—to create a new leadership for the school.

Acknowledgments

In 1989, I began work on a series of books for Jossey-Bass that together would make the case for creating a new educational administration, with a new vision of leadership and a new theory for the school. *Moral Leadership* was published in 1992, and *Build-*

ing Community in Schools was published in 1994. This book completes the trilogy. Throughout the writing of the three books, I have relied on bringing together the thoughts and practices of countless teachers and administrators who are struggling to make schools better places for living and learning. To all of them I am deeply grateful for what I have learned. My students at Trinity University, the wonderful principals in our Principals' Center, and my faculty colleagues also deserve mention. They have provided me with the longest-running "post-doc" experience in history. The time I spent as a visiting practitioner at the Harvard Principals' Center in the fall of 1994 was critical in helping me to bring this particular book together. I want to thank Millie Blackman, the director of the center, and the many principals at the Harvard center with whom I had the privilege of talking. And finally, I want to thank my long-term colleague Robert J. Starratt, whose thoughts loom large between the lines of this trilogy of books.

San Antonio, Texas   Thomas J. Sergiovanni
June 1995

The Author

THOMAS J. SERGIOVANNI is Lillian Radford Professor of Education and Administration at Trinity University, San Antonio, Texas. He received his B.S. degree (1958) in elementary education from the State University of New York, Geneseo; his M.A. degree (1959) in educational administration from Teachers College, Columbia University; and his Ed.D. degree (1966), also in educational administration, from the University of Rochester.

From 1958 to 1964, he was an elementary school teacher and science consultant in New York state and taught in the teacher education program at the State University of New York, Buffalo. In 1966, he began nineteen years on the faculty of educational administration at the University of Illinois, Urbana-Champaign, where he chaired the department for seven years.

At Trinity University, Sergiovanni teaches in the school leadership program and in the five-year teacher education program. He is senior fellow at the Center for Educational Leadership and the founding director of the Trinity Principals' Center. A former associate editor of *Educational Administration Quarterly*, he serves on the editorial boards of the *Journal of Personnel Evaluation in Education, Teachers College Record, Catholic Education: A Journal of Inquiry and Practice*, and *The Journal for a Just and Caring Education*. Among his recent books are *Moral Leadership* (1992), *Building Community in Schools* (1994), *The Principalship: A Reflective Practice Perspective* (1995), *Rethinking Leadership* (1999), and *The Lifeworld of Leadership: Creating Culture, Community, and Personal Meaning in Our Schools* (2000).

Leadership for the Schoolhouse

Chapter One

What We Have, What We Need

Most teachers and administrators are trying to make schools better places of learning for students. Yet progress has been frustratingly slow. Pasco County, Florida, Principal Robert Dorn (1995) explains:

> Our district has tried numerous strategies: we lifted a school day; we increased time on-task; we increased the graduation requirement; we mandated exit testing; and we put in a no-driver's-license-if-you-drop-out provision. Many other school-boards have tried instituting similar enhancement policies. Locally we try to deal with attendance and discipline rules, but these measures alter the nature of the system without addressing the root causes of the problem. We have audited our rules for compliance purposes. What needs to be examined now is the unhappy consequence of these efforts: there have been no significant improvements in student achievement patterns. These innovations have failed to eliminate poor instruction and ineffective and redundant curricula. This raises the question of exactly what our professional roles are going to be to help more students become prepared for a new century [p. 7].

As a result of his recent study on high school restructuring, for example, Gordon Cawelti (1994) observed that while one can point to changes here and there, the more traditional ways of doing things still dominate the scene. A recent Rand Study (Bimber, 1994) stated that "The movement toward experimentation with the principle of de-centralization shows every sign of continuing to accelerate. Yet the results so far are not encouraging. There is little evidence of better student achievement, and few schools calling themselves 'de-centralized' have made major changes in established educational practice" (p. vii). And further, "The case studies support the hypothesis about de-centralization's failure to cause change. Evidence from the three public schools shows that there is not much variation in the nature of decision-making under different degrees and forms of de-centralization at these schools" (p. 46). Bimber concludes that the primary reason for the limited impact of decentralization is the inability of school districts to deal with the inseparability of decisions. Decisions deal with different subjects, all of which are interdependent. Yet the decision-making structures represent fragmented attempts to deal with one or another issue, but not all of the issues at the same time.

Michael Fullan (1994) observed recently that neither the first wave of reform (with its top-down strategies) nor the second wave of reform (with its bottom-up strategies) have worked very well. In his words, "In short, centralized reform mandates have a poor track record as instruments for educational improvement. This failure has led some to conclude that only de-centralized, locally driven reform can succeed. Site-based management (SBM) is currently the most prominent manifestation of this emphasis. So far, however, the claim of superiority of grass-roots initiatives is primarily theoretical. In reviewing evidence on site-based management [reported in Fullan, 1991, p. 201] . . . I concluded that restructuring reforms that devolved decision making to schools may have altered governance procedures, but did not affect the teaching-learning core of the schools" (p. 187).

Fullan argues for approaches that blend top-down and bottom-up strategies in new ways. He may be right, but I'm not sure. He does offer an important clue, however, as to how changes that stick can be introduced in schools. The evidence, as he sees it, points to "re-culturing" leading to "re-structuring" more effectively than restructuring leading to reculturing. The two of course interact in a way that one feeds into the other. Nonetheless, it appears that changing school structures, and introducing new management systems, quality designs, and decision-making strategies are less the means by which school cultures change, and more the *results* of changes in the school culture.

Culture is an important factor in improving schools. Less obvious is the connection between culture and theory. The heart and soul of school culture is what people believe, the assumptions they make about how schools work, and what they consider to be true and real. These factors in turn provide a *theory of acceptability* that lets people know how they should behave. Underneath every school culture is a theory, and every school culture is driven by its theory. Efforts to change school cultures inevitably involve changing theories of schooling and school life.

When we think about schools, do we have the right theories in mind? I don't think so. Despite commitment and will, this is the reason why it is so hard to improve schools over the long term. Your response might be, "Does it really matter if we don't have the right theories? After all, most of us are involved with problems of the real world, and theories don't seem very relevant to our daily practice." Theories often don't seem very relevant. But the theories I am talking about are practical ones. They are practical because they influence what we see, how we think, what we come to believe to be true, what we say, and how we behave. They function like mindscapes by providing us with images of reality that dictate the terms within which we must live, and that define for us what is and is not the case. Our theories, in other words, have led us to create the kinds of schools we now have. And if we want to change them, we have to start by creating new theories—theories that fit better the context of schools, and fit better what schools are trying to accomplish. Let's observe how some of the theories we now have work by visiting a portion of life in Crestwood Elementary School. The story is real, but the people are identified by pseudonyms.

New teachers to Crestwood are assigned a mentor who provides support, helps with problems, and in other ways tries to make that difficult first year of teaching a successful one. When Theresa arrived at Crestwood as a new special education teacher, she was introduced to Arturo by the district's director of special education. Arturo had been an outstanding special education teacher at another school prior to becoming Crestwood's assistant principal the previous year.

Theresa and Arturo hit it off from the beginning. They decided to begin their mentoring relationship by having Arturo teach the class for a while. Together they designed the classroom to accommodate his teaching style. Theresa became an "understudy" not only by observing Arturo's teaching, but by trying to understand the subtleties of his teaching, his intent, his style, the ways in which he seemed to bring together curriculum, teaching, and learning environment for specific purposes.

From the beginning of their relationship, Arturo and Theresa were engaged in a continuous conversation about what was going on in the classroom. Arturo was interested in having Theresa focus on how he used teaching arrangements and learning designs to influence students' behaviors. He believed that issues of control are best handled informally rather than by direct intervention. Theresa was able to observe firsthand just how this could be accomplished.

Next it was Theresa's turn to take over the class. Theresa understood that what made sense for Arturo might not make sense for her. She had to change the way the classroom was set up, and to think about teaching and learning arrangements in ways that fit her own style, needs, and intents. As Arturo explains, "Theresa was not lacking in ideas. She decided, for example, that the existing furniture wasn't very suitable for how she wanted to work with the students. It happened that too many tables were ordered for one of the kindergarten classes, and I was able to get ten of those tables for Theresa's class. The students helped us redecorate the classroom, and it turned into an amazingly lively place. The students all created their own little areas, and each area included an aquarium. These aquariums served as living science exhibitions. Students brought such organisms as turtles, tadpoles, spiders, insects, plant life, and algae, and maintained these exhibitions physically, and also by keeping logs of their experiences in working with their mini-museums."

Arturo made frequent informal visits to Theresa's classroom. Each was followed by an open conversation about what was going on, about issues, and about other events that were of interest to Theresa. From time to time, Theresa experienced some difficulties with her teaching. On one occasion, it was her inability to reach a particular child. On another occasion, it was a classroom management problem. In every case issues were dealt with openly. Arturo was also there for her when nonteaching problems arose. "One day Theresa brought a note from a parent for me to read. The parent was very hostile towards her. She wanted my advice as to how to respond. She prepared a response, and shared it with me, but I felt that it sounded too defensive. After pointing this out,

I suggested she replace a short phrase with one of my own. She was both amused and relieved with the suggestion, and used it with great success. She was very, very appreciative."

Theresa was delighted when Arturo shared several of the lesson plan books he had accumulated over the years as well as his daily logs, notes, and boxes of other materials that he had used when teaching. Theresa found these to be a treasury of inspirational and useful ideas. Clearly, Theresa and Arturo were off to a good start in their mentoring relationship.

I wish this story could end here. But shortly before the end of the first semester, the relationship between Theresa and Arturo cooled. In the beginning, it didn't matter that Arturo was the assistant principal. But as time went on, some of the other teachers at Crestwood asked Theresa whether she realized that sooner or later Arturo would be the person who would have to evaluate her. When evaluation time did come, Arturo scheduled a meeting with Theresa, and explained the process. The meeting was a "preconference" of sorts that wound up being stressful for Theresa. Arturo did everything that he could to try to make her feel at ease, and assured her that evaluating with the required state instrument would be little more than a *pro forma* process. He was more interested in conducting an evaluation that would serve as a benchmark for where Theresa was, and that would be helpful to her as she planned ahead. But Theresa was unconvinced. Two days later she requested that the mentoring relationship be discontinued.

In Arturo's words, "It was obvious that our relationship was changing. I had picked up on a few hints, but I wasn't sure until then. I talked to Theresa, and asked her if she would feel comfortable writing me a letter telling me what the problem was from her perspective. 'I want you to be honest with me, and tell me how I might help things get back to where they were.'" Arturo received the following letter:

> Dear Arturo:
>   Last week I had a chance to discuss a wide variety of classroom frustrations with our associate psychologist when she came by for an ARD [admission, referral, dismissal] meeting. It was valuable, and it made me remember how useful it was talking to you

about similar concerns. It's a shame that I have to wait for these visits when your good advice is just down the hall, but I feel uneasy in seeking your counsel in our present respective positions. This is a disappointing aspect of our job relationships, which I'm sure frustrates you as much as me.

Although I still value your advice, I know that your obligations to other teachers and to administrative goals sometimes makes it hard for you to assist me in the way you used to. In your present supervisory position, I feel uncomfortable asking you about the challenges I often face in my classroom. It is difficult for me to share information, and speak in full candor, when I know that I must also maintain a professional level of control and preparation for observation and evaluation.

When we talk about my class, and you offer suggestions or theory, I can't receive your advice in the same casual way I used to. As my supervisor, your suggestion carries more weight, and I must treat it as a directive. You had suggested I post classroom rules. I decided not to. If you advise me to do this now, I would post them the next morning. This seems unfortunate, for we often need to explore several paths before choosing a successful course. I wish we could share a cup of coffee, and have a discussion about my class without thinking about future evaluations. I know that my class would benefit.

Please keep offering what advice you can under the circumstances. I will do my best to talk with you freely, in spite of professional concerns. Let me know if you have any good solutions to this dilemma.

Sincerely,
Theresa

What has happened to Theresa? Why has her relationship with Arturo taken this all-too-familiar turn? Theresa has learned about the script of schooling, and the role this script requires her to play. The other teachers at Crestwood are veteran actors who have memorized the script, and play their parts so naturally that they don't think much about it anymore. This is just the way schools are.

According to this script, you can't get too cozy with administrators because they might turn things around on you at evaluation time. Once Theresa became socialized to the norms of the existing culture, she behaved similarly. This script became part of her mindscape of reality.

Though most of us find the events described above regrettable, we are reluctant to challenge some basic assumptions behind the theory of leadership that leads us to think about supervision and evaluation in this way. Arturo, after all, is the assistant principal. Theresa needs to accept that, and at the same time trust Arturo enough to know that he will help rather than hurt her; that she will be treated fairly, and so on. What is not questioned is the *why* question. Arturo's obvious competence notwithstanding, why do we assume that teachers should automatically be evaluated by principals or other supervisors? The answer is that our present theories assume that hierarchy equals expertise. In many instances, this is indeed the case. After all, knowledge about teaching and learning—and ability to share these insights with teachers—is a key factor in any good principal-selection process. But few would argue that one is better able to evaluate everyone else who is lower in the hierarchy just because of her or his position. Many of us wonder why we have to think about hierarchies in schools this way in the first place.

Our theories of school leadership shape the way we think about these and other issues. Instead of questioning them or changing them, we work hard to fix them up in an effort to get them to work better. We insist, for example, that principals be *the* instructional leaders in schools and be *the* managers, cheerleaders, and motivators of teachers. And we provide them with training to get them to do their jobs better. We could just as well assume that teachers themselves must be the instructional leaders in schools, and we could just as well assume that they have a responsibility to become self-managing. This would mean accepting more responsibility than is now the case for supervising and evaluating each other, for looking after their own continued professional growth, and for meeting their commitments to school purposes.

In this scheme, the role of school principal would remain important, but would take on an investment character aimed at purposing and capacity-building. Less emphasis would be given to doing things for teachers and more emphasis would be given to helping teachers do things for themselves. Though direct leadership might have to be used initially, the overall goal would be to make this kind of leadership less necessary. But this approach requires the development of a new theory of schooling that rethinks how the burdens of responsibility and accountability should be shared, and that provides a new understanding of what leadership is and how it works.

What would such a theory look like? For starters, a new theory might abandon the assumption that one's bureaucratic role in the school determines her or his functions. Functions could just as well follow patterns of expertise as patterns of hierarchy. If that were the case at Crestwood School, it would not be unusual for competent Arturos to mentor fledgling Theresas or for Theresa's fellow teachers to have a major say in her tenure decision.

However, a new theory of this kind would have to acknowledge that there are other legitimate sources of authority than the traditional bureaucratic ones, or the traditional personal leadership ones. It would need to recognize that position power and expert power are often not shared by the same person, and yet both have rightful roles to play in schools. And such a theory would have to provide for new and better ways to connect people to each other, and to their work, than our present emphasis on management systems and quality designs allows. But new theories are hard to accept.

In the *Republic,* Plato explored the idea of being a captive of one's mindscapes in the famous allegory of the cave. Imagine being one of many living in a cave, chained in place so that you cannot move. At the opening of the cave, a large fire casts shadows of people onto the walls. You and the other cave dwellers believe the shadows to be real. You give them names, and talk to them. In Plato's allegory, one of the dwellers is allowed to leave and venture into the real world. Suppose you are this person, and now you must return to the cave. You understand that the shadows are a mere reflection of a more complex reality. You try to share your new mindscape of the world with your fellow cave dwellers, but they do not believe you. Indeed, they find your new views threatening. They turn inward even further to preserve the familiar. Having rejected your views, they begin to reject you. If you are strong willed, you manage to hold your own against the force of group norms. But there is a good chance that over time you will come to see the shadows of the cave once again in the old way.

Social scientists, too, have documented how our mindscapes trap us into thinking and believing in certain ways. Thomas S. Kuhn (1970), for example, describes the famous research of Bruner and Postman (1949) to make this point. Subjects were asked to identify a series of playing cards including some normal cards and some that were doctored (a red six of spades and a black four of hearts, for example). Without hesitation, subjects identified the doctored cards as normal. When the anomalies were pointed out, most of the subjects were resistant, and some held out to the end of the experiment without compromising their original labeling. Kuhn (1970) notes "a few subjects . . . were never able to make the requisite adjustment of their new categories. Even at forty times the average exposure required to recognize normal cards for what they were, more than ten percent of the anomalous cards were not correctly identified" (p. 63).

What are the theories of leadership and schooling that provide us with the script of roles and lines we are forced to play and say as administrators, teachers, parents, and students? What are the theories that determine how we organize schools and see to their operation? What are the theories that determine how we think about and provide school leadership? What are the theories that shape the decisions we make about how to hold people accountable? Three theories developed for the business world compete for our attention: the Pyramid Theory, the Railroad Theory, and the High Performance Theory.

The Pyramid Theory and the Railroad Theory have been around for a while. Both are deeply embedded in the decisions that we make about schooling. The High Performance Theory caught our attention during the early eighties with the publication of the best-selling management book *In Search of Excellence* (Peters and Waterman, 1982). This is the theory that fills the pages of popular leadership books and magazines, provides the topic of trendy workshops, and is the hallmark of school improvement strategies espoused by many educational consultants, school administrators, and state education officials who seek to restructure our schools.

We'll get back to it later, after discussing the other two theories, which are older and more deeply embedded in our approach to schools as organizations.

On the surface, the Pyramid Theory seems deceptively simple. The way to control the work of others is to have one person take responsibility by providing directions, close supervision, and inspection. As the number of people to be supervised increases, and as separate work sites develop, it becomes impossible for one person to do everything directly. Management burdens must therefore be delegated to other managers. A hierarchical system begins to emerge with the head manager at the top, other managers with delegated power just below, and those to be managed at the bottom. Rules and regulations develop as the top manager attempts to ensure that all the managers think and act as they should, and that those who are to be managed at the bottom are all treated similarly. These rules and regulations provide the protocols and guidelines to be used for planning, organizing, controlling, and directing.

In time, what seemed like a simple process of one person directing the work of others evolves into a complex management system that ensures a certain order is established and maintained, and that whatever the organization accomplishes or produces meets a common standard. The Pyramid Theory works well for many kinds of organizations. It is particularly suited to organizations that need to produce standardized products in uniform ways, and to situations where deviations hinder rather than promote effectiveness. But when the Pyramid Theory is applied to the wrong situation, the result is a bureaucratic nightmare. When applied to schools, for example, the work of principals and teachers becomes increasingly simplified and standardized, and the outcomes of schools also come to share these features of simplicity and standardization.

The Railroad Theory seeks to control the work of people who do different jobs, meet different responsibilities, and work in different locations by standardizing the *work processes* they engage in. Instead of relying on direct supervision and the visible display of hierarchical authority, a great deal of time is spent anticipating all the questions and problems that are likely to come up. Once this is done, answers and solutions are developed that represent tracks people must follow to get from one goal or outcome to another, or from one place to another. Once the tracks are laid, all that needs to be done is to teach people how to follow the tracks, and to set up a monitoring system to confirm that everyone follows the tracks and reaches the various stations on time.

The Railroad Theory works in jobs that lend themselves to predictability and determination. Work processes are standardized by specifying in great detail what needs to be done, when, and by whom. The "one best way" to get the job done is spelled out, and a system of monitoring is put into place to make sure that workers are following directions and meeting expectations.

When the Railroad Theory is applied to schools, an instructional delivery system is created. Specific objectives are identified and tightly aligned to an explicit curriculum. Typically, both are connected to a specific method of teaching. Teachers are supervised and evaluated and students are tested to ensure that the approved curriculum and teaching scripts are being followed.

Scripting the work scripts the worker as well. As schooling becomes more routinized and impersonal, teaching and learning becomes more "teacher-proof" and "learner-proof." Soon *functional rationality,* the primacy of rules following, displaces *substantial rationality,* the primacy of goal-oriented decision making (Mannheim, 1940). Principals, teachers, and students are rewarded for following rules rather than solving problems, for following procedures rather than making good decisions, for doing things right rather than doing right things. Though no one intends that bureaucratic teaching and learning be the result of the Railroad Theory, it soon comes to dominate the lives of principals and teachers, teachers and students, and schools and parents.

In both the Pyramid and Railroad Theories, it is important for managers to be sensitive to workers as human beings by ensuring a pleasant working environment, and by doing what they can to meet the psychological needs of workers. Applied to schools, principals are expected to be expert human relations practitioners who know how to handle people by pressing the right psychological buttons to get the job done, while keeping morale up.

The High Performance Theory departs radically from the Pyramid Theory and the Railroad Theory by de-emphasizing visible top-down hierarchies, and de-emphasizing the detailing of scripts that program what people do. Instead, decentralization is the key word as workers are empowered to make their own decisions. Sometimes this empowerment is individual, with each person being free to make his or her own decisions about what to do. Sometimes it takes the form of *shared decision making,* as groups of workers join together to make decisions.

The issue of control found in the Pyramid and Railroad Theories remains. But the way one gets control in the High Performance Theory is not by connecting people to rules or scripted work, but by connecting people to outcomes. Borrowing from the lessons that Peters and Waterman (1982) and their successors learned from excellent business organizations, the High Performance Theory assumes that the key to effective leadership is to connect workers tightly to ends, but loosely to means. As we shall see, this principle is seminal to today's school restructuring efforts.

When the High Performance Theory is applied to schools, ends are considered to be measurable learning outcomes. With learning outcomes standardized, everyone is expected to produce similar results. Schools, however, are free to decide how they are going to achieve the outcomes or produce the results. Teachers and principals are given the freedom to organize their schools and to teach in ways that they think will best enable them to meet the standards that are provided from above. The High Performance Theory also emphasizes collecting data that gauges how well workers are doing, and encourages them to figure out ways in which they might continuously improve the quality of their own performance and that of their organization.

Once principals and teachers are empowered to make decisions about how they will do the assigned work, it is assumed that they will be more motivated, committed, and satisfied. The formula for success is as follows: High Performance goals combined with high performing workers will result in high performing learning for students.

The ideas behind the High Performance Theory seem more plausible and appealing than the "monitor them carefully, make them happy, and they will comply" ideas associated with the Pyramid and Railroad Theories. But issues remain. First, will the discretion over means that empowered teachers and schools have provide sustained results over time? Or will the choice of means become increasingly narrowed by the official and standardized outcomes? Will the narrowing of means lead to *de facto* scripting (teaching to the test, for example) of the work of teachers and students? Second, while discretion over means might initially provide principals, parents, and teachers with a new sense of responsibility and new feelings of efficacy, will these feelings sustain themselves over time? Or does true empowerment and a full sense of responsibility require having autonomy not only over means, but over ends as well? Are schools—and the administrators, teachers, parents, and students who identify with them—empowered when they do not have direct control over purposes, goals, priorities, and other issues of policy?

The Pyramid, Railroad, and High Performance Theories have important lessons to teach us. They provide understandings that can help us to make better decisions about leadership for the schoolhouse. But underneath, the three theories share common features that make their application to schools in a systematic way inappropriate. In all three, schools are understood as formal organizations. Understanding corporations, armies, research laboratories, transportation systems, universities, government bureaus, and fast-food restaurant chains as formal organizations makes sense. But the organization metaphor does not fit the nature of school purposes, the work that schools do, the relationships needed for serving parents and students, the context for work that teachers need to be successful, or the nature of effective teaching and learning environments.

A key principle in formal organizations is the separation of functions by roles. Both the Pyramid and Railroad Theories separate the *planning* of how work will be done from the *doing* of it. This separation of the two may be okay in running a chain of fast-food restaurants, but not in running a school, where professional discretion is essential to success. Separating the planning from the doing isolates teachers from each other, and from the needs of their students. It also fragments the work of teaching—and this fragmentation, in turn, separates meaning from learning for students.

Within the High Performance Theory, those who have to do the work get to decide how to do it, and this is an important improvement over the other two theories. But problems of isolation, fragmentation, and loss of meaning remain, *because planning what to do is separated from planning how to do it.* Not only is professional discretion compromised, but so are democratic principles. Few parents and teachers, for example, are likely to feel empowered by being involved in decision-making processes that are limited to issues of management.

The High Performance Theory also gets better scores than the Pyramid and Railroad Theories on how people should be treated. But at root all three theories rely on another characteristic of organizations, the bartering of rewards and punishments for compliance as a way to connect people to each other and their work. Bartering leads to calculated involvement. Schools, however, do not work well when people are connected to each other and when people are connected to their work for calculated reasons. Instead of treaties and contracts, schools need compacts and commitments. Instead of calculated connections, schools need moral connections for things to work well.

The emphasis on bartering and calculation stems from the incomplete assumptions about the nature of human nature that are inherent in the three theories. The three assume, for example, that principals, parents, teachers, and students are motivated principally by self-interest, and thus are out to maximize their gains and cut their losses. This assumption is embodied in the heavy reliance on the use and denial of incentives and other kinds of rewards to motivate people. And all three theories assume that human beings make decisions about what to do individually. Each person looks for the deal that best serves her or his own individual interests.

For schools to work well, we need theories of leadership that recognize the capacity of parents, teachers, administrators, and students to sacrifice their own needs for causes they believe in. We need theories of leadership that acknowledge that parents, teachers, administrators, and students are more norm-referenced decision makers than individual decision makers. Instead of making individual calculations based on self-interest, we should acknowledge that people are responsive to norms, values, and beliefs that define the standard for living together as a group and that provide them with meaning and significance.

Rarely are any of the three theories implemented alone in schools. Instead, their pattern of use seems to be developmental. Instead of replacing older theories completely, each newcomer on the scene becomes an add-on to its predecessors. Some schools rely on a combination of the Pyramid and Railroad Theories. Other schools add High Performance Theory to the first two.

Often ideas from Total Quality Management (TQM) are included in the High Performance Theory. On several occasions in this book I will use TQM as a metaphor for theories and management schemes that we have indiscriminately imported to education. TQM has been widely embraced by experts in school management and organization. By contrast, its advocates are rarely experts in the *core technology* of schools—experts who seek to improve schools by focusing on teaching and learning, curriculum design, and evaluation. To this latter group of experts, issues of governance, school structure, and leadership are important, but decisions about them should be the natural consequences of decisions about core technology, and not the other way around.

The views of Richard S. Prawat, a leading teaching effectiveness researcher, are representative of how core technology experts think about TQM and other dimensions of the High Performance Theory. Prawat's research represents a social constructivist's view of learning, and provides a rationale for understanding classrooms and schools as learning communities. Prawat (1993) states:

> Based on an examination of TQM, I have concluded that this approach—or, indeed, any approach based on a business metaphor of schooling—is inconsistent with the social constructivist view of learning. Let me explain why . . . TQM like all management models is based on a process of rational problem solving. . . . Once the goals have been identified, the manager is responsible for identifying the best available means to achieving these goals. Finally, a system is put in place to audit both the practice and the product. In TQM, the manager joins with the workers in the continual analysis and improvement of the work process. In all of the above, the organization takes its cue from the "customers" it serves. In the case of schools, this includes parents, school board members, tax payers, and local businessmen [p. 8].

Prawat believes that schools have little to gain by adopting enlightened business practices. Schools are just too different. Their purposes are different, the people they serve are different, the work conditions needed to serve effectively are different, and the relationships needed to serve effectively are different. Learning communities thrive on commitment, and make decisions in process as events unfold. According to Prawat, enlightened business practice, by contrast, focuses

> on rational problem solving, and the concomitant control orientation, may interfere with the development of commitment. The problem with rational problem solving is that it's an excessively convergent process. It assumes that one can identify which goals reflect best practice at the outset of the change process. . . . Rational problem solving, the process which underlies TQM and other management models, closes off discussion just at the point where it might yield fruitful results. It also pulls administrators out of the process. Their role is to implement the agreed upon plan; they are expected to stay comfortably above the fray, a stance which inhibits the free flow of information [p. 9].

To Prawat, the goal of learning communities is to build social and intellectual connections among people, and control interferes with this process. "People who view themselves primarily as managers, as men or women of action, who 'make things happen,' who 'shake things up'—these people are ill-equipped to play the role required of someone who builds a learning community. The person who builds a learning community might better be described as a 'child or adult developmentalist,' someone who knows where he or she stands on the issues; someone who has a well developed theory of teaching and learning based on the best current work in education" (p. 9). School leaders, Prawat maintains, need to be comfortable enough with issues of teaching and learning, and comfortable enough with parents, students, and teachers to engage in the kind of give and take that is necessary for the school community to construct a shared understanding of what it is about, and what it is trying to accomplish.

Though often described as a "paradigm shift" in thinking, at its base the importation of TQM to schools keeps in place the key principles and structures that embody traditional management theories. For example, the importance of strong and consistent leadership from "top management" is a prominent theme in the literature of TQM. Bonstingl (1992, p. 42) believes that this is the most important characteristic of a quality school. Quality, TQM advocates believe, cannot be delegated. Responsibility for processes, systems, and outcomes must remain with top management. This stance, prominent in the Pyramid, Railroad, and High Performance Theories, makes much sense in many business organizations, but does it make sense in medical clinics and other professionally oriented enterprises? Does it make sense among church missionaries, school teachers, and other groups where being self-managing is so important to success? Or should responsibility for quality in these enterprises and settings be shared? In a new theory of leadership for the schoolhouse, not only principals and teachers but parents and students too must accept their share of responsibility for assuring quality.

Total Quality Management relies too much on systems that have been carefully crafted by top managers who function as visionary leaders. According to its edicts, it is top management that must strive to put into place the right quality system. According to Bonstingl (1992), "Quality products in schools, as in businesses, come from quality processes," and quality processes come from adopting a systems/process orientation (p. 41). But, as Fullan (cited in O'Neil, 1994) points out, "It's individuals who are going to be the solution to education reform, not systems" (p. 2). Fullan believes that real reform will come about as a result of individuals with a clear moral purpose working together on issues that are meaningful to them. In his words, "Too many organizations, too many systems, have gotten diverted by trying to develop the vision and the mission statement up front, as if you could 'get it right' and then implement it." Fullan believes that systems are best for maintaining the status quo, not for bringing about real change. "Systems have a good track record for keeping things the way they are, [they] . . . don't have a good track record for changing things. Individuals have that track record" (p. 2).

The development of the Pyramid, Railroad, and High Performance Theories, and their adaptation as models of school leadership, closely parallels their evolution in the business sector. New ideas are first espoused in the pages of *Business Week,* and later find themselves in the pages of *Education Week.* The themes found in the best-selling business books soon come to dominate the pages of both school administration and school reform books. Business consultants who spread the word in the corporate sector spin off educational consultants who then spread the same word in the school sector. Professional organizations then join the fray, creating a new training industry that soon saturates the field with the adopted-for-schools business practices. Sadly, this pop management literature often finds its way into the academic journals, and soon becomes part of the official literature of educational administration—a predicament that does not characterize the literature in teaching and learning, educational psychology, and other education disciplines.

Many educational reformers believe that the more closely our ideas are linked to the world of business, the more credible they are for application to the world of teachers and children, of teaching and learning, of parents and schools. Indeed the enthusiasm for borrowed business models is often summed by the following statement, paraphrased from one made by a leading educational consultant: "Bringing quality to school requires the same innovative leadership that is found in effective business organizations. What the world's competitive economy requires of our businesses, society must require of our schools. It is time for schools to join the quality revolution."

The issue for us is not business people, but business models. Business leaders have played key roles in such national reform efforts as The Next Century Schools initiative, The Essential Schools movement, and The New American Schools Development Corporation. In San Antonio, for example, the business community has taken the lead in the San Antonio 2000 School Reform effort, and business leaders play key roles in the reform work of Trinity University's Center For Educational Leadership. This pattern of local business persons providing leadership and other assistance in school reform is common across America.

Few business leaders, however, want to send their own children to schools that are organized in such a way that they require the application of the Pyramid, Railroad, High Performance Theories—or any other business theory—to function effectively. Most prefer to send their own children to schools that function more like families, learning communities, and moral communities. This is why so many business leaders (and political leaders too) choose to send their own children to smaller, more intimate, more family-like, more personable, yet more challenging religious and nonreligious independent schools. When they do choose a public school for their children, it typically shares the same community features of independent schools.

Though adopting business *models* for use in schools can be troublesome, ideas from business are often useful in helping us think through our problems, clarify the issues we face, and find solutions. But there is a difference between adopting and learning. There is a difference between adopting and adapting as a result of that learning. And there is a difference between borrowing a theory from business and picking up some ideas that can help us to invent better, albeit unique, theories for the schoolhouse.

Total Quality Management, for example, is a management strategy that advocates claim is based on the philosophy of W. Edwards Deming. A thoughtful reading of Deming reveals that he was a communitarian at heart who felt that moral purpose was important to workers, and that they would respond to leadership that provided it. His philosophy resonates with that of John Dewey, and provides a source of inspiration and ideas for use in schools. But Deming's philosophy and TQM as practiced in the corporate world and imported to schools are as different as day and night. Maurice Holt (1993), who writes compellingly on this topic, notes:

> As a first step, we might profitably banish the use of the word *quality* in descriptions of any Deming-inspired reforms. It's a word that Deming himself uses sparingly, and never in such expressions as "total quality management," a phrase he dislikes. Central to Deming's thought is the notion of *variation,* and to suggest "total management" of anything seems to deny the existence of forces that inexorably affect any institutional environment. The adjectival use of *quality,* in any event, has virtually become ironic, since it is now applied universally to anything saleable (a newspaper ad, for example, tells the reader to "do your part in saving water by installing a quality automatic sprinkler system"). The word has become debased coinage and can only be used in an explanatory context, as when Deming writes: "What is quality? A product or service possesses quality if it helps somebody and enjoys a good and sustainable market" (for quality is, in any case, a moving target; vacuum tubes give way to transistors). When used to label reform proposals, *quality* has little meaning other than to lend a vicarious Deming-like aura to the enterprise [p. 7].

Corporate Cultures (Deal and Kennedy, 1982) provides another example. This book shows readers how the metaphor "culture" can be a useful frame for understanding leadership and life in corporations and other enterprises including schools. Culture is a metaphor adopted from the disciplines of sociology, anthropology, and moral philosophy, where it refers to the values and rituals that provide people with continuity, tradition, identity, meaning, and significance, as well as to the norm systems that provide direction and that structure their lives. Deal and Kennedy provide an interpretation of this concept of culture suitable for business organizations. They recommend that business leaders construct contrived cultures that rally workers around themes of corporate loyalty. This involves leaders inventing artificial rites and rituals, celebrations, traditions, and the like that stimulate the feelings and loyalties found in real cultures. Companies that do this, Deal and Kennedy reason, will have workers who are more committed and more productive.

The Deal and Kennedy book is helpful to us because it raises the cultural issue in a practical way. We learn that schools too could be understood differently and more fully by using a cultural frame of reference. We also learn a great deal about the dynamics of individual and group behavior, and about the power of norms, from reading their descriptions of the cultures of various corporations.

Learning lessons and borrowing models, however, are not the same. Instead of borrowing the concept of culture from corporations, or even trying to adapt this concept, we need to go straight to the original sources—to the disciplines of sociology, anthropology, and moral philosophy. The analogy of primary and secondary sources fits here. Corporate culture is a secondary-source concept. It is an interpretation by business writers of a primary-source concept. Learning about how experts from other fields such as business interpret a primary source and use it for *their* unique purposes can help us with our own interpretation. But if we don't construct our own interpretation for schools from the primary source, then we wind up with a *tertiary*-source set of concepts and practices that too often do not fit school purposes and school settings.

Our interpretation of culture and our adaptation of this concept to school practice should emphasize the building of authentic communities where values are rooted in the democratic and Judeo-Christian traditions that define our nation, and where values reflect our commitment to school purposes and ideals. Our interpretation should not emphasize the construction of contrived cultures. Chapter Five, "The Roots of School Leadership," discusses the problem of using tertiary-source ideas in school leadership further, using vision and using transformational leadership as examples. The primary source for vision, for example, is religion ("Where there is no vision, the people will perish" Proverbs 29:18). And the primary source for transformational leadership is moral philosophy (Burns's 1978 notion of elevating followers to higher moral levels). But since we in education borrowed both vision and transformational leadership from the business literature (from secondary sources, in other words) the original meanings have been lost in our tertiary-source interpretations for and applications to schools.

This wholesale borrowing of theories from other fields has resulted in a characterless literature of educational administration. Character is something that cannot be imported from General Motors, Xerox Corporation, Du Pont, or some other place. Character is something we must create for ourselves. The decisions we make, for example, about how quality should be defined in schools, and about how we should work to achieve it, should be the natural consequence of our struggles to make schools better. Our quest for character does not begin with some other field's models, but with our own visions of what we want for the parents and students we serve, of how we want to work together to achieve these purposes, and of what we need to do for purposes and beliefs to be embodied in our school practice.

But what about the restructuring efforts of a number of blue-ribbon companies? For example, what about Goodyear Tire and Rubber Company's experiments with "supervisorless teams" and "self-directed work groups"? What about shared decision making efforts at Procter & Gamble, American Express, and IBM? What about the downsizing and decentralizing at Xerox? Didn't David Kearns (1988) tell us that schools should follow his example at Xerox by making "central office administration a service center. Go ahead and allocate funds, but the principal and staff will be responsible for spending them. . . . this will streamline middle-management . . . and it will put resources where they belong, in the school building" (p. 24). These are great ideas, of course, but are they ideas unique to or invented by business? After all, Catholic schools have been operating with lean central office staffs for years.

In 1988, for example, the Roman Catholic Archdiocese of New York had a central office staff of 27 (18 professionals and 9 secretaries) serving 322 schools and 114,000 students for a ratio of 1 staff member for every 4,200 students. (In New York City schools, by contrast, the ratio of central office staff to students was 1 for every 147 students) (Fiske, 1988). Writing in 1983, Joe Nathan noted that Chicago's Catholic schools with 250,000 students employed only 35 administrators as compared with public school figures of 3,500 administrators for 500,000 students. Religious and nonreligious independent schools have always been known for empowering their teachers, and in many small public schools, teachers and parents work merrily together as self-directed work teams.

The point is, few corporate restructuring ideas are original. In fact, such ideas as downsizing, empowerment, and self-managing behavior and the like are part of our democratic legacy as promulgated by the American founders, and embodied in such sacred documents as the Declaration of Independence, the Constitution, the Bill of Rights, and the Federalist Papers. The roots of this legacy were found in the democratic traditions of ancient Greece.

Following the teachings of Aristotle and Plato, the American founders envisioned a nation bound together by a set of values, and a common creed that would define the citizenship as a *polis*. Their key ideas included the building of a consensual and morally held understanding of obligations on behalf of common goals and the common good, combined with a commitment to individual freedom within this web of obligations. The Declaration of Independence, for example, guarantees to all persons the self-evident truths of equality, life, liberty, and the pursuit of happiness, and government based on the consent of the governed. And the Bill of Rights reminds us that for these truths to indeed be self-evident, we must accept the obligation to embody them in our thoughts and behaviors.

David Clark and Judith Meloy (1989) argue that if we were to renew our commitment to this democratic legacy as the foundation for schooling, schools would operate on the basis of:

- Democracy

- Group authority and accountability

- Variability, generality, and interactivity in work assignment

- Self-discipline and control exercised individually and collectively

- Group commitment to and consensus about organizational goals and means [p. 292].

Given what is already going on in religious and independent schools, and in many small public schools, and given this democratic legacy that provides a foundation for life in the United States, it seems self-serving for business writers and their educational imitators to assume that downsizing, empowerment, and other organizational virtues have their origins in the corporate world.

Admittedly, reclaiming our democratic legacy and creating our own theory and practice of school leadership is the more difficult way to go. It is much easier to start with an imported list of principles to implement, or with imported models for reforming schools, than with a vision of reform that leads us as educators to invent our own practices of leadership. Despite the difficulty involved, our ability to improve schools depends on our ability to create a unique leadership for the schoolhouse. We cannot have one without the other.

We have much to learn by looking beyond the schoolhouse. But where we look makes a difference. Some places are more "school friendly" than others. Some places are richer than others in providing for our democratic legacy. These places evoke images of leadership, organization, and behavior that fit better the school's world of children, of learning, of development.

School-friendly sources for new ideas are rich with organic metaphors that depict natural and living phenomena. Families, neighborhoods, churches, and even flocks of birds, bee colonies, weather systems, and other natural enterprises and phenomena are examples. Less friendly sources, by contrast, are filled with images of structural-functional systems embodied in formal organizations. Corporations, armies, transportation systems, and other artificial enterprises and phenomena are examples. Imagine that it's time for you to send your own child or your own grandchild off to kindergarten. As you and the child look ahead to the next thirteen years, which set of images for the school do you feel most comfortable with, the natural organic ones, or the artificial structural-functional ones?

Chapter Two

A Theory for the Schoolhouse

"This was more like a survey. A test is when you sit at a desk, you don't talk and you answer the questions—otherwise you fail," stated a fourteen-year-old boy. Another youngster remarked, "These aren't questions that are right and wrong. It's just what kids think." And a third noted, "I think all the money they spent on these tests should have been spent on buying English books that we could read during our classes" (Shuster, 1994, p. 1–B). The students were complaining about the new California Learning Assessment System (CLAS) Tests they had just taken. The tests are designed to assess higher-order thinking, ability to solve problems, and conceptual understanding of subject matter.

The CLAS tests are admittedly controversial. No doubt they have problems that need fixing. Interesting, nonetheless, are the theories of schooling revealed in the complaints of these three students—theories countless other students have also internalized. Learning, it appears, has little to do with how one thinks, or whether one understands, but with right and wrong answers. Assessment is about following directions, answering questions, and passing or failing. And a good lesson is one that involves reading textbooks in class. The theories seem strikingly at odds with the kind of schooling envisioned in such reports as SCANS, the Secretary's Commission on Achieving Necessary Skills (U.S. Department of Labor, 1991). SCANS details what the world of work requires from schools. Its recommendations are echoed in dozens of other governmental and foundational reports that urge schools to focus on how one learns, on increasing academic standards by encouraging conceptual understanding, on teaching less content but expecting higher levels of mastery, and on insisting that students demonstrate what they know rather than just answer multiple-choice questions on tests.

Students too, it appears, have learned to recite today's script of schooling so well that it has become second nature. One of the reasons that today's theories are so entrenched is that teachers, principals, and parents have left the question of theory for the schoolhouse up to others. Perhaps the feeling is that if you ignore something long enough, it will go away. After all, who has time for theory, when involved in the day-by-day requirements of schooling? But theories don't go away. Instead, like the slowly boiling water that cooked the proverbial frog, they creep up on us. And before long, they control our lives.

Most readers who are familiar with the New Testament remember the story of the vine and the branches. "I am the vine, you are the branches . . . apart from me you can do nothing" (John 15:4–5). This image captures the theory problem we face in schools. In education, the vine represents the various theories of schools understood as formal organizations, and the branches are the way schools work as a result. We can prune the branches to control growth. And we can graft new varieties of branches onto the vine to change its bounty and its appearance. But over time the vine shapes the branches to its own image, and produces fruit on its own terms.

The story of the vine and the branches can be read between the lines of a number of social science theories that speak to the same theme. The concept of uncertainty absorption, the tendency to understand new ideas in old terms (March and Simon, 1958), and the tendency for already established categories to shape the meaning of new understandings (Mannheim, 1940) are examples. After decades of attempts to reform schools by introducing shared decision making, management by objectives, flexible scheduling, team teaching, year-round schools, Total Quality Management (TQM), and other management systems, basic school structures remain in place, and basic assumptions about leadership and learning continue to ensure that the old school realities endure. To change these realities, the DNA of the vine itself must be altered.

Let's suppose that we are DNA splicers. Our goal is to create a new theory of leadership for the schoolhouse. Before we begin our work, we decide to search for criteria that can be used to determine what we should consider for our theory. This chapter presents some ideas to help get us started. They are offered to encourage discussion, and to invite you to propose some criteria of your own.

I believe a theory for the schoolhouse needs to be aesthetically pleasing. Its language and images, for example, should be beautiful, and should evoke thoughts that are consistent with the school's human purposes and condition. I believe that a theory for the schoolhouse should be idea based, and emphasize moral connections. It should evoke sacred images of what goes on, and should compel people to respond for internal rather than external reasons. I believe that a theory for the schoolhouse should be responsive to the full nature of human rationality. I believe that a theory for the schoolhouse should provide for decisions about school organization and functioning, curriculum, and classroom life that reflect constructivist teaching and learning principles. I believe that a theory for the schoolhouse should strive to transform the school into a center of inquiry—a place where professional knowledge is created in use as teachers learn together, solve problems together, and inquire together. And I believe that a theory for the schoolhouse should encourage principals, teachers, parents, and students to be self-managing, to accept responsibility for what they do, and to feel a sense of obligation and commitment to do the right thing.

Suppose we were to accept this or a similar list of criteria. Would our present leadership policies and practices still be adequate, or would we have to invent new ones for the schoolhouse? Try answering this question as each criterion is elaborated below.

Aesthetic Qualities

A theory for the schoolhouse should be aesthetically pleasing. Its language and images need to be right for students, right for the kind of work that schools do, and right for the kinds of purposes that schools have. The reasons why aesthetic qualities are important can be illustrated by a thought exercise. Below are examples of statements written in two voices—one from the literature of TQM, the example we used in Chapter One, and the other from the literature on gardening. Both have implications for schooling. As you read the voices, however, which of the two speaks most clearly to you? To which of the voices would the parents and teachers in your school respond most positively?

Let's begin with the voice of TQM, a frequent add-on for those who seek to reform schools by using the High Performance Theory. In a recent analysis of over fifty new books on quality, Snyder (1994) reports:

> Six themes emerge that can provide educational leaders with a framework for becoming "quality driven": 1) *Client satisfaction* is the focus for work within the entire "quality" organization; 2) *top level leadership* for quality drives organizational change; 3) *thinking in terms of "systems,"* and recognizing the interdependence of functions, programs and services, enables the organization to respond quickly to needs; 4) *strategic planning* is essential for improving quality; 5) *continuous training* and collaboration and use of data systems empowers workers to meet challenges routinely; and 6) *continuous improvement* through quality, as viewed by the customer (through numerous data gatherings and analysis strategies) becomes a way of life [p. 3].

In one of the books reviewed (Murgatroyd and Morgan, 1993), the following statements appear. They are representative of much of the TQM literature. "Total quality means what it says. All aspects of the organization have to be dedicated to the goal of achieving the highest possible standards of performance as required by their customers (internal or external), given the strategy they are pursuing. This dedication is not to be merely a rhetoric, but defined by specific required standards of performance. It is total, in that it affects all who work in the school and in that it affects all activities undertaken in the name of the school" (p. 60).

Key to TQM is the systematic management of a number of customer-supplier relationships. Teachers, for example, are both customers and suppliers, as are students, principals, parents, and so on. The suppliers for teachers as customers include students who supply completed schoolwork, and administrators who supply a proper working environment, information about students, induction, training, and teacher evaluation. Teachers are suppliers to an array of customers including students who receive teaching and learning outcomes, a proper classroom climate, evaluation, counselling and mentoring, and even compassion and love. Teachers supply administrators with various outcomes, parents with timely reports of student progress, and so forth. In TQM the customer-supplier relationship is the basis for all school activities. Murgatroyd and Morgan explain:

> The customer-supplier relationship within the school and between the school and its consumer and provider stakeholders are the basis for all activities. If these processes and chains are managed well, with a constant focus on high performance and improvement, then quality achievements follow. What is important here is that attention is given to the managing of *processes,* because processes produce outcomes. Far too much attention has been focused on securing outcomes, no matter what the process looks like—yet it is process quality and effectiveness that leads to *sustainable* quality outcomes. Process here refers to the way in which people work to achieve results [p. 60].

Let's now turn to the voice of gardening. Below are some comments from a gardening article that appeared in a local newspaper (*San Antonio Express News,* 1994, p. 18–A). The article provides four secrets of success to introducing a child to gardening:

> Don't make gardening into work, especially initially. Weeding beds, mowing lawns, and raking leaves can come later. The first experiences should be fun and/or dramatic ones, such as planting seeds, pulling carrots, hunting for four-leaf clovers or making a necklace from daisy flowers.

> If a child expresses an interest in gardening, let him have his own small garden plot. If the plot is too big, gardening will seem too much like work. Mark the plot as separate from the rest of the garden, and let the young gardener plant whatever it is he likes to eat, even if it's just cucumbers and corn.

> Go through a seed catalogue with a youngster and point out all the weird or unusual plants you find. (Few youngsters will be able to resist showing interest in purple-podded string beans that turn green when you put them in boiling water, or White Wonder Tomatoes that are sweet and productive, but white instead of red, or blue potatoes that taste great.)

[Gardener Mary Jo Phillips advises that] the best way to encourage kids to garden is not to specifically encourage it. Making a big fuss over anything makes kids suspicious of your motives, so it rarely works. All you really have to do is be interested yourself. Then a love of gardening and the natural world becomes a neat grown-up activity that you, of course, are kind enough to let them in on, instead of some deadly educational project.

On first read the voice of gardening may seem strange. It is, after all, simply stated, natural, and uncomplicated. For these reasons, we might be tempted to ask, "As professional educators, shouldn't we look to logically argued and technically oriented prose such as is represented by the voice of TQM, rather than to folksy gardening language?" Before making up our minds, let's submit the two voices to the Bill and Barbara Test (Mintzberg, 1982).

Henry Mintzberg, one of North America's most respected management authorities, was invited to review the chapters of an edited book on leadership. The book was supposed to "break the mold," and carry the field "Beyond Establishment Views." He asked Bill and Barbara, two practicing business managers, to read the articles and comment on them.

Bill had this to say: "Many presentations go to incredible and convoluted lengths and explanations, only to finish by stating the obvious. Complex and over-inflated jargon is often used to camouflage emancipated ideas. Many seem more interested in studying the subtleties of a particular research approach—or even worse, studying other studies—than they are in contributing to a real understanding of leadership itself." And Barbara commented as follows: ". . . if these contributions are an indication of the current state of leadership research, then the gulf between academia and the real world is even greater than I feared. What bothered me most, as I read the presentation, was the gnawing suspicion that all the research was being carried out as an end in itself. Hence, relevance was really a side issue. Perhaps I am being too much of a pragmatist, but I persist in thinking that research even in academic circles should mean something." Both Bill and Barbara then provided a chapter-by-chapter analysis of the book. In short, the book failed the Bill and Barbara Test.

In commenting on Bill and Barbara's verdict, Mintzberg (1982) points out that the issue is not one of research versus practice, or of other simplistic dualisms. He states, "I believe in pure research—that having to come up with a 'how to' conclusion can spoil a useful line of thinking, but I have also discovered that intelligent practitioners are as interested as researchers in the results of pure research. . . . So long as the results have some relevance to their own concerns. And are expressed in clear English. I have never come across a good insight in organizational behavior management that could not be so expressed. Jargon is too often a smoke screen that clouds the emptiness of the findings. The Bill and Barbara Test is designed to blow it away" (p. 248).

Compare, for example, the earlier comments on TQM with the following plain English summary of an important research study on academic and motivational characteristics of nine- and ten-year-olds:

> Children whose mothers encourage them to be curious, to persist, to master new tasks, and to take pleasure in learning tend to have higher academic achievement than those whose mothers use rewards or punishments to encourage school success.
>
> So concludes the study by three California State University researchers that appeared in the March issue of the *Journal of Educational Psychology*.
>
> Adele Eskeles Gottfried, James W. Fleming, and Allen W. Gottfried interviewed the mothers of a hundred and seven children, and assessed the children's academic and motivational characteristics at ages nine and ten.
>
> They found that nine-year-olds who were internally motivated to do well in school had mothers who had encouraged that attitude. Moreover, those children's academic achievement at both nine and ten was greater than it was for peers whose mothers had encouraged academic success with rewards and punishments.
>
> In fact, the researchers found, such external motivational practices tended to have a negative effect on children's motivation [Viadero, 1994a].

One striking difference between the voices of TQM and of educational research is that the latter actually says something useful about teaching, learning, and schooling. The TQM comments, by contrast, seem more concerned with process than substance, and generic process at that.

What do managers want the leadership literature to tell them? According to Mintzberg, "Managers want to know how . . . they themselves can lead more effectively. But it is not only advice they need. Perhaps not even primarily advice, at least from us as researchers. They need insight—startling insight, ideas that will change their perceptions. With such insight, they—or the staff people and consultants close to them say they . . . will know what to change. How many of the presentations . . . in the research journals over the past ten years, properly translated, provide that kind of insight? How many would you give to the managers you know—say to your dean [or superintendent], to help him serve you more effectively? Better still, how many would you take to heart if *you* became dean [or superintendent]?" (p. 249).

To Mintzberg, simple prose and the right images help provide the needed insight. He notes that in Abraham Kaplan's monumental work *The Conduct of Inquiry* (1964) aesthetic quality is listed as a criterion that should be applied in assessing the validity of theories. Kaplan wrote, "Sometimes a scientist needs courage, not only of his convictions, but also of his esthetic sensibilities" (1964, p. 319). Following Kaplan, Mintzberg (1982) concludes that "If a theory is not beautiful, then the odds are good that it is not very useful" (p. 250).

It is now time for you to conduct your own Bill and Barbara Test by sharing the TQM and gardening examples with the parents and teachers in your school. Let them choose the one that they find most appealing—most useful. Neither sample is comprehensive enough or developed enough to provide us with a theory. But samples are revealing nonetheless, and I am betting that they will reveal a clear preference for gardening talk over TQM talk, for aesthetic sensibility over structural hyper-rationality. If the comparison was between the voices of educational research and TQM, the results would be the same. Parents and teachers would express a clear preference for substance over process, for school talk over generic talk. I believe that W. Edwards Deming, the management philosopher and strategist whose ideas TQM advocates claim as supporting their work, would agree with the parents and teachers. After all, he did not believe that either the literal or metaphorical use of the word "customer" was appropriate for schools. He often stated that "We don't have customers in education" (Holt, 1993, p. 23).

Moral Connections

I believe a theory for the schoolhouse should be idea based, and emphasize moral connections. It should evoke sacred images of schools, and should compel principals, teachers, parents, and students to be self-managing.

All theories of leadership emphasize connecting people to each other, and all theories of leadership emphasize connecting people to their work. Connections satisfy the needs for coordination and commitment that any enterprise must fulfill in order to succeed. The work of teachers, for example, must fit together in some sensible way for school purposes to be realized, and teachers must be sufficiently motivated to do what is necessary. But not all theories emphasize the same kinds of connections.

The Pyramid, Railroad, and High Performance Theories all emphasize contractual connections. They assume that teachers are motivated primarily by self-interest, and act as individuals to negotiate an exchange settlement with others and with the school that best meets their needs. For schools to get teachers to work together, or to do the things that need to be done, rewards must be traded for compliance and penalties traded for noncompliance. A similar pattern of rewards and penalties characterizes life within classrooms as teachers and students engage in trades.

Extrinsic rewards are likely to be emphasized in the Pyramid and Railroad Theories. The High Performance Theory, by contrast, tends to emphasize intrinsic rewards along with extrinsic. Intrinsic rewards are aimed at the satisfaction of higher-order needs for recognition, autonomy, achievement, self esteem, and so on. But trades are trades, and as a result leadership inevitably takes the form of bartering. "Leader and led strike a bargain within which the leader gives the led something that they want in exchange for something the leader wants" (Sergiovanni, 1990, p. 30). Bartered deals inevitably lead to calculated involvement. When involved for calculated reasons, students study hard as long as they get desired rewards, and teachers go the extra mile for the same reasons. But when rewards diminish or lose their attraction, effort levels decline.

We need a theory of leadership based on moral connections. Moral connections come from the duties teachers, parents, and students accept, and the obligations they feel toward others, and toward their work. Obligations result from common commitments to shared values and beliefs. Moral connections are grounded in cultural norms rather than in psychological needs. For this reason, they are stronger than extrinsic or intrinsic connections.

Once established, shared obligations, common commitments, and accepted norms represent substitutes for interpersonal leadership. The sources of authority change from heavy reliance on bureaucratic or personal leadership to heavy reliance on moral leadership. What teachers do, for example, depends much less on what leaders do to them and much more on their own self-management.

Leadership based on bureaucratic authority seeks compliance by relying on hierarchical roles, rules, and systems expectations. Leadership based on personal authority seeks compliance by applying motivation theories that meet psychological needs, and by engaging in other human relations practices. By contrast, leadership based on moral authority relies on ideas, values, and commitment. It seeks to develop a shared followership in the school—a followership that compels parents and principals, teachers and students to respond from within.

Images of Rationality

I believe that a theory for the schoolhouse should be responsive to the nature of human rationality. *Rational,* according to Webster, implies the ability to reason in a logical way, and the ability to draw conclusions from inferences. Too often, however, theories of leadership for the schoolhouse, and their accompanying management descriptions, are judged to be rational based on how they look or sound, rather than on evidence that they are effective.

The Pyramid, Railroad, and High Performance Theories, for example, differ in how they function stylistically. But they all propose that key to the development of school improvement strategies is to start by emphasizing *ends* first. Once ends are determined, the next step is to figure out the *ways* in which they will be accomplished. Finally emphasis is given to working on the *means* to follow the ways by identifying, training, supervising, and motivating people. High Performance Theory tries to combine the second and third steps by empowering workers through shared decision making to help management figure out the ways, and this is some-

times mixed in with the process of training, supervising, and motivating to help them do the job.

The ends-ways-means approach (and the theories that prescribe it) works well for enterprises where work patterns can be
described as linear, and the language of linearity does have rational appeal even if it doesn't wind up being rational in practice.
Though it may sound counterintuitive, a more effective, and thus
more rational strategy for schools (and other enterprises whose
work patterns are more nonlinear than linear) is to adopt a means-
ways-ends approach (Hayes, 1985; Sergiovanni, 1987a). Concen-
trate on people first. Build them up by increasing their capacity
to function and by increasing their commitment. Link them to
purposes, and help them to become self-managing. Then con-
centrate on ways by letting them figure out what to do and how.
Finally, focus on the ends that they decide to pursue, ensuring
that ends are consistent with shared purposes, values, and commitments.

The means-ways-ends approach allows people to choose goals
and paths as they go along. Choosing as one goes is important
because the world of school practice is nonlinear. And as Gleick
(1987) points out, nonlinearity means that the act of playing the
game has a way of changing the rules. In nonlinear situations,
every decision changes existing conditions in such a way that suc-
cessive decisions also made at the same time no longer fit. This
makes it difficult for a principal, for example, to plan a series of
steps or to be committed to a stepwise set of procedures based on
the initial assumptions. Once the context changes, the original
sequence just no longer makes sense (Sergiovanni, 1991). In short,
nonlinear relationships between events lead to consequences that
are unpredictable.

Hayes (1985) points out that deciding where to fit people into
the planning process influences what happens in important ways.
And the decisions we make about this issue depend on the images
of human rationality we believe to be true.

Let's explore different images of rationality by taking the following inventory. Exhibit 2.1 presents three statements summarized from Shulman (1989, p. 171). All three are true to a certain
extent, but some are more true than others. Using a total of ten
points, distribute points among the three to indicate the extent to
which you believe each to be true.

Exhibit 2.1. Three Aspects of Rationality.

1.   People are rational; they think and act in a manner consistent with their goals, their self-interests, and what they have been rewarded for. If you wish them to behave in a given way, make the desired behavior clear to them, and then make it worth their while to engage in it.

_____ pts.

2.   People are limited in their rationality. They can make sense of only a small piece of the world at a time, and they strive to act reasonably with respect to their limited grasp of facts and alternatives. They try to construct their own individual definitions of situations rather than passively accept what is presented to them. If you want to change them, engage them in active problem solving and judgment, don't just tell them what to do.

_____ pts.

3.   People are rational only when acting together; since individual reason is limited, men and women need opportunities to work together on important problems, thus achieving through joint effort what individual reason and capacity could not accomplish. If you want to change people, develop ways in which they can engage in the change process jointly with peers.

_____ pts.

Total _10_ pts.

The first image of human rationality fits the Pyramid and Railroad Theories very well. This image is also prominent in the High Performance Theory. High Performance Theory also gives some attention to the image of rationality portrayed in the second statement, but this emphasis is an add-on to the first image. None of the three theories emphasizes the third image.

Both the second and third images of rationality emphasize helping people to make sense of their world. Sense-making occurs when people are able to construct their own definitions of situations, and are involved with leaders in active problem solving. The second image assumes that much of this meaning-making is an individual endeavor as people struggle alone to simplify the world around them; find concepts, values, and principles that they can hang on to; and create realities that they can live with.

The third statement portrays an image of collective rationality. This image recognizes that humans are not so much individual decision makers as they are norm-referenced decision makers. Amitai Etzioni (1988), a compelling challenger of the views of motivation and rationality that characterize traditional management theory, points out that our emotions count as much as our rationality, as do our preferences, values, and beliefs, and also the social bonds with which we identify. Though it often appears we are functioning as individuals who seek to maximize personal gain and minimize personal loss, we are in reality influenced by norms. We take into account what important others think and believe, and how they will react to our decisions. We have, as Bellah and his colleagues (1985) point out, an innate ability to be connected to each other, and to cooperate with each other in pursuit of needs that emerge from a shared conception of our common human nature.

Recently I asked forty successful principals and superintendents to assess the images of rationality presented in Exhibit 2.1, using a 10-point scale to indicate the extent to which each was seen as true. Out of a total of 400 points, they awarded 106 to the first image, 123 to the second image, and 174 to the third image, for an average per image of 2.5, 3.25, and 4.25 points respectively. Though this survey is informal, it has some interesting implications. It suggests that, in a new theory of leadership for the schoolhouse, the second and third images of rationality need to be placed at the center, and the first image needs to be moved to the periphery. Doing this acknowledges the importance of sense-making, and provides for the expression of collective rationality as parents and principals, teachers and students live and work together in schools.

Constructivist Principles

I believe that a theory for the schoolhouse should provide for making decisions about school organization and functioning, curriculum, and classroom life that are based on constructivist teaching and learning principles. Designing practice from constructivist principles requires fundamental changes in the ways in which we think about school leadership.

Most readers know the adage "form should follow function, or function will change to follow the form." Since the Pyramid, Railroad, and High Performance Theories are all imported to the school context, they provide us with ready-made forms for organizing schools, scheduling classes, developing curricula, planning for teaching and learning, and providing supervision, staff development and evaluation. With ready-made forms, our job as administrators, reformers, and teachers is to figure out how we can craft goals and objectives and develop environments and strategies for teaching and learning that fit these forms. Though in principle everyone believes that form should follow function, in practice we still continue to alter function to fit our imported forms.

Adopting a constructivist perspective inverts this form-function equation. Instead of beginning with a form for schooling, and trying then to fit what we are trying to do into the categories provided, we begin with what we know about teaching and learning, and what we want to accomplish for children and parents. With these as the framework, we then design outward, seeking to create forms of organizational structure, curriculum, and teaching and learning that fit the functions.

Constructivist research, as we shall see in later chapters, tells us a great deal about how children and adults learn. It reveals that the second and third images of human rationality discussed in the last section best account for how we think and how we learn both in and out of school. In Shulman's words, "contemporary thinking about learning borrows from two recent traditions: humans as boundedly rational, and humans as collectively rational. The more complex and higher-order the learning, the more it depends on reflection—looking back—and collaboration—working with others" (1989, p. 174).

Constructivism is not a theory of teaching that enables us to design down to how students learn. It is instead a theory about knowledge and a theory about learning that enables us to design out to teaching as well as out to issues of school structure, organization, and teacher development. At root is the simple idea that children and adults construct their own understandings of the world in which they live.

To constructivists, the metaphor "learning community" provides a conceptual frame for this design work. As Prawat (1993) explains, "current research on learning, joining on the work of cognitive psychologists and cultural anthropologists . . . [has] changed the focus of our attention in education—away from an individual differences approach in teaching and toward one that focuses on developing a learning community in the classroom" (p. 8). He elaborates: "If learning is a social act, more akin to the process of socialization than instruction (Resnick, 1990), the criteria for judging teacher effectiveness shifts from that of delivering good lessons to that of being able to build or create a classroom 'learning community'" (Prawat, 1992, p. 12). Constructivist principles point to how adults learn. And for this reason they are helpful in sorting out issues of collegiality, action research, and teacher development as well as issues of teaching and learning for children.

Center of Inquiry

I believe that a theory for the schoolhouse should strive to help the school become a center of inquiry. Over twenty years ago, Robert J. Schaefer (1967) gave the ninth annual John Dewey Society Lecture, "The School as a Center of Inquiry." This seminal work provides the impetus for much of the new literature on teacher development, professional community, and school-based "action" research. To Schaefer, "the school must be more than a place of instruction. It must also be a center of inquiry—a producer as well as a transmitter of knowledge" (p. 1).

Traditional theories of schooling view schools as instructional delivery systems, and teaching as being similar to playing a game of baseball. Specific learning objectives are defined, and teaching is directed to these objectives. The teacher is the pitcher who throws teaching strikes into this learning outcome zone. Because some pitches miss the zone, they are declared balls, and don't count in the final score. Inservice education and supervision focuses on increasing the possibility that teachers will throw the required strikes. Teacher evaluation keeps track of the numbers of balls and strikes that are thrown.

This view of teaching persists even though the evidence suggests that the game of teaching may be more like surfing than baseball. If, for example, the strike zone were to change its definition, then pitches that were originally strikes might not be, and those that were balls might be safely inside (Sergiovanni, 1987b). The baseball metaphor just doesn't fit. In practice, teachers learn to ride the wave of the teaching pattern as it unfolds, accommodating to shifting circumstances. When riding the wave, models of teaching and learning are used rationally to inform intuition and enhance professional judgment, and not in a hyper-rational way to prescribe practice. Teachers create their strategies in use as they teach, taking into account unique contexts and changing circumstances. They abandon a "one best way" teaching approach in favor of crafting unique strategies that fit the circumstances they face.

With surfing as the metaphor, teaching is viewed less as the delivery of instruction, and more as a problem-solving activity. Students are not objects of instruction, but participants in the teaching and learning process. To engage in teaching as surfing, teachers must constantly inquire into their craft, searching for the knowledge needed to deal successfully with the circumstances at hand.

Schaefer points out that "it is not only our need for new knowledge, but also our responsibility for the intellectual health of teachers which suggests that schools should be conceived as centers of inquiry. When divorced from appropriate scholarship and substance in pedagogy, teaching resembles employment as an educational sales clerk, and ceases to be a more than humdrum job. . . . By concentrating upon the distributor function alone, the school effectively imprisons rather than liberates the full power of the teacher's mind" (p. 2).

A theory for the schoolhouse should provide the conditions that allow the school to become a center of inquiry. It should provide answers to such questions as: What kinds of organizational structures, teaching environments, and working conditions are needed to allow and encourage teachers to engage in the work of inquiry as they teach? To become researchers of their practice? To become reflective practitioners? The Pyramid, Railroad, and High Performance Theories are not able to answer these questions very well because they bring to the schoolhouse preconceived forms with ready-made answers. It is these answers to which all questions must be shaped. In a new theory for the schoolhouse, we must begin with the premise that inquiry is at the heart of the work of the teacher, and then design out from this premise to the conditions of schooling needed to enhance this work.

Self-Managing Goals

I believe that a theory for the schoolhouse should encourage principals and teachers, parents and students to become self-managing, to accept responsibility for what they do and to feel a sense of obligation and commitment to do the right thing.

Proposing a new theory for the schoolhouse that provides for the development of self-managing people is an idea that few resist. But how do we accomplish this end? Many look to Chaos Theory for the answer. From Chaos Theory comes a burgeoning and useful literature on self-managing systems and learning organizations—places where people can become self-organizing and self-developing. I believe we can learn a great deal from Chaos Theory, but I do not believe that Chaos Theory can be used to develop a working theory for the schoolhouse.

Let us see what we can learn. Chaos theorists study the behavior of living systems, coming up with fascinating results (Gleick, 1987). Recently, for example, I read an account of how honeybees solve the problem of finding and exploiting the best food sources available (Morse, 1992). Their success, it seems, depends upon the behavior of individual bees who make their own independent decisions rather than on some kind of a hierarchical structure within the colony, on the specification of bee production quotas that ultimately become bee production scripts, or on bees working collaboratively to make shared decisions about where to hunt.

Bees, it appears, rely on entrepreneurship as a form of self-management. They function as a group of independent operators with each bee making her own decisions as to which flower patches to work. They assess the richness of the nectar source, and engage in a dance that communicates to others whether this level of richness is low or high.

Bees are not picky about who is doing the dancing, but only about what the message is. Thus experienced foragers are treated the same as bees with little or no experience. As Morse (1992) explains, "What is now understood is that this is sufficient to direct the actions of the whole colony. A bee being recruited follows one dancer, and takes the advice of this bee, and forages accordingly. She then makes her own decision as to the profitability of the food source, and may dance herself, or not, and continue to forage at the site, or not, depending upon what she thinks. The bees that dance longer are more likely to be encountered, and to recruit more bees. In this way the greatest number of bees get the best advice, and forage at the best site."

The hive is able to achieve order from the actions of many independent bees; this is the message that appeals to those who try to apply Chaos Theory to schools. Bees are self-managing, and together comprise a network of individual actors that act independently and yet in unison, without guidance from any central control. They are not a mere collection of individuals engaged in parallel play, but are tied together somehow into a colony of individual actors engaged in common purposes.

Despite the appeal of these images, Bee Theory raises more questions than it answers. Such factors as instinct and unusual forms of communication that may be genetically determined explain much of bee behavior. Still, it is clear that bees, termites, and other colony insects don't follow predetermined plans, and that the hive or nest as a whole engages in a self-organizing process where order emerges from chaos. And it is clear that this image provides a useful way for us to think about developing a new theory for the schoolhouse.

The issue, however, is one of connections. How do we get students and teachers, parents and principals to connect to each other in authentic and meaningful ways? How can people become tied together not only interpersonally, but spiritually as well? The answer, in part, is to share a common moral quest—to be tied as one to a set of shared conceptions, purposes, ideas, and values. Bees connect alright, but the connections for bees are too limited to satisfy the rich, complex demands of human nature.

The science of human behavior concerns itself not just with our biological and psychological natures, but with our cultural nature as well. Basic human urges and drives, fundamental needs, and patterns of conditioned learning are examples of our biological nature as are our perennial concerns for growth, maintenance, and reproduction. Complex urges and drives, higher-order needs, and emotions themed to introspection that shapes our personalities are examples of our psychological nature. Both biologically induced and psychologically motivated behavior can, I believe, be explained by Chaos Theory, and both can be motivated by the development of self-managing systems. The application of Chaos Theory to schools breaks down, however, when we get to the cultural side of human nature—the side that allows us to believe, to sacrifice, to strive for goodness, to be motivated out of altruism, to care for ideas and principles, to be moral persons.

A theory for the schoolhouse must look beyond bee behavior and other Chaos Theory metaphors for self-managing systems to an image of the school that places moral authority at the center. Needed is a cultural theory that moves people by the force of compelling ideas and by the force of shared values. Needed is a cultural theory that understands shared norms as being more important than psychological need fulfillment as the impetus for motivation. Needed is a cultural theory that views the school as a moral community, the theme of the next chapter.

Chapter Three

Understanding and Building Community in Schools

In *Leadership in Administration* (1957), Philip Selznick compares "organizations" with "institutions," pointing out that the latter are invariably more successful in providing for the needs of members and in accomplishing purposes. Selznick, who is now professor emeritus of law and sociology at the University of California, Berkeley, states that organizations are made up of standard building blocks that lend themselves to manipulation by administrators who are interchangeable across all organizations, and whose practice involves the use of generic theories, concepts, and skills. As a result, their roles are generalized to the point that they become similar to parallel roles in other organizations. From an organizational perspective, managing a shoe store, bank, insurance company, hospital, day-care center, church, school, or family successfully all require the same insights, know-how, and skills. The consequence of adopting this generic approach is a lapse in integrity, and a loss of character that leads to undifferentiated organizations and mediocre performance. By contrast, institutions are more successful enterprises because they maintain integrity and character by being *unique in their purposes,* structures, and ways of doing things.

Selznick has put his finger on a problem we face today as we seek to improve schools by using theories about generic organizations. In his words, "The design and maintenance of organizations is often a straightforward engineering proposition. When the goals of the organization are clear-cut, and when choices can be made on the basis of known and objective technical criteria, the engineer rather than the leader is called for" (p. 137). Despite the best of intentions, too often superintendents, principals, and teachers wind up functioning as engineers rather than as leaders. Why is this so? Because over time it is not leadership but engineering that organizations want and thus reward. This is a lesson that many school people who try to be leaders learn very quickly. The crux of this dilemma is that today's theories of organizations push us to function as engineers even though we know that it is not engineering but leadership that schools need to improve. The challenge of leadership is to resist this pressure, whatever the costs. And the ultimate purpose of *school* leadership is to transform the school into a moral community. The restoration of integrity and character in school administration depends on this transformation.

We can appreciate better the urgency of changing our theory of schooling to moral community—and the urgency to invent a unique practice of leadership that fits this theory—by having a look at what happens when organizational thinking is applied to everyday school problems and issues. Consider, for example, the following sequence of real events, summarized from Sergiovanni (1995):

Terry, a high school principal in a large city, was recently "demoted" to assistant principal and transferred to one of the district's junior high schools for violating teacher evaluation procedures. Teachers are required to be evaluated with an instrument containing roughly fifty teaching behaviors while teaching a fifty-minute lesson. The principal's job is to record the behaviors the teacher demonstrates, and to note whether the observed behaviors are of exceptional or ordinary quality. Evaluations must be conducted according to a specific timetable.

Terry never got around to formally evaluating Chris using the required instrument. As a result of many informal visits, however, Terry was aware of Chris's teaching style. During the last week of school, Chris reminded Terry that the required evaluation had not been conducted. Since the deadline had already passed, Terry (with Chris's permission) completed an evaluation form using actual examples of teaching she had observed over the semester. The form was signed, and sent up the chain.

Violating established teacher-evaluation procedures was judged to be a serious enough matter to warrant demoting and transferring Terry. Two other principals had committed similar violations of teacher-evaluation rules and regulations and were disciplined in the same way. Consistent enforcement, the district reasoned, is a cardinal principle of good management. Rules must be universally applicable and consistently enforced with the same consequences—a point reinforced by the district's legal counsel.

From one perspective, it is hard to fault the school district's decision. Violating teacher-evaluation procedures is serious business. Rules are rules and they must be followed. Consistency is important to maintain discipline; everyone must be treated the same. Individual circumstances cannot be taken into account or the system will fall apart. This is just the way it is. This is good management. That is, this is what good management is as defined and understood by the theory of organization that dominates how we think and what we do.

Terry was completing her first year as principal. Most observers credit her with "having turned the school around." She is known by most of the teachers and nearly all the students as a loving and devoted principal. An article in the local paper noted that parents and students credit Terry with transforming morale at the high school by taking a personal interest in students and instilling a positive attitude. This article quotes a student as saying, "She knows most of us on a first-name basis, and she'll call you personally."

An editorial reported that about 200 parents and students appeared at the school board meeting to show their support for Terry. It stated, "In this day of gangs and dropouts, how many inner-city schools would have such a turnout of students and their families to back a principal? When someone inspires students and helps them care about school, should a paperwork infraction bring that special relationship to a halt?" Given the theory of organizations that now defines what school management is and how it works, the answer to that question is Yes, a paperwork infraction should indeed bring this special relationship to a halt. Moreover, because two other principals were punished in this way for the same infraction, the school had no choice but to treat Terry the same.

Receiving a different answer to the question requires a change in the theory itself. If, for example, schools were understood as communities rather than as formal organizations, Terry's story would be quite different. Universal rules and consistent application of rules are not that important in communities. Each case is more likely to be treated individually. Communities are more likely to place values over rules and to evaluate situations in a more open-ended way than was the case with Terry. Indeed, if schools were understood as learning communities and caring communities, Terry might even emerge as a hero rather than a villain. Whether a principal is considered to be a hero or a villain, it seems, is a function of the theory that is used to define and prescribe appropriate practice.

When all enterprises are managed and led the same way, none are managed and led very well. Whatever the nature of the enterprise, those that are able to function with integrity and character create structures and engage in activities that are uniquely adapted to their purposes and to their societal roles. They develop distinctive ways of making decisions, distinctive commitments to their purposes and distinctive ways of operating, and distinctive connections to the people they serve. In Selznick's words (1957), "In this way the organization as a technical instrument takes on values. As a vehicle of group integrity, it becomes in some degree an end in itself. This process of being infused with value is part of what we mean by institutionalization. As this occurs, *organization management* becomes *institutional leadership*. . . . The building of integrity is part of what we have called the 'institutional embodiment of purpose' and its protection is a major function of leadership" (pp. 138–139).

Selznick's Theory of Institutional Leadership provides a major breakthrough in understanding the way societies, organizations, and institutions work, and has much to contribute to the way schools should be viewed. Institutional leadership seeks to bring integrity to an enterprise, and seeks to transform the enterprise from an organization to an institution. As the process of institutionalization occurs, schools evolve away from generic organizations and become distinctive communities. This evolution to community provides the school not only with a distinctive character, but with a defense of integrity that allows the school to develop a distinctive competence.

How are communities different from organizations? Communities are organized around relationships and ideas. They create social structures that bond people together in a oneness, and that bind them to a set of shared values and ideas. Communities are defined by their centers of values, sentiments, and beliefs that provide the needed conditions for creating a sense of "we" from the "I" of each individual.

In communities, members create their lives with others who have similar intentions. Both organizations and communities must deal with issues of control. But instead of relying on external control measures, communities rely more on norms, purposes, values, professional socialization, collegiality, and natural interdependence. As community connections become established in schools, they become substitutes for formal systems of supervision, evaluation, and staff development.

The ties of community also redefine how empowerment and collegiality are understood. In organizations, empowerment is understood as having something to do with shared decision making, site-based management, and similar schemes. Within communities, empowerment focuses less on rights, discretion, and freedom, and more on commitments, obligations, and duties that people feel toward each other and toward the school. Collegiality in organizations results in part from administrative arrangements that encourage or force people to work together, and in part from the team-building skills of principals. In communities, community members are connected to each other for such moral reasons as mutual obligations, shared traditions, and other normative ties, so collegiality is something that comes from within.

A Theory of Community for Schools

In *Building Community in Schools* (1994), I brought together ideas, examples, and experiences with community from many sources into a framework that could help principals, parents, and teachers in their struggle to build community. Since community means different things in different disciplines, I proposed that for schools we define the term as follows: *Communities* are collections of individuals who are bonded together by natural will and who are together bound to a set of shared ideas and ideals. This bonding and binding is tight enough to transform them from a collection of "I's" into a collective "we." As a "we," members are part of a tightly knit web of meaningful relationships. This "we" usually shares a common place and over time comes to share common sentiments and traditions that are sustaining.

I then proposed that the concepts *gemeinschaft* and *gesellschaft* could help us understand this definition and the forms it might take as schools become communities. The use of foreign words can seem pretentious, but this risk is worth taking. *Gemeinschaft* and *gesellschaft* are special words in sociology that communicate a set of concepts and ideas that are well known in that discipline. When a sociologist observes that one group of individuals, one town, or one school is more *gemeinschaft* than another, those familiar with the terms have a detailed image of what is meant.

Gemeinschaft translates to community and *gesellschaft* to society. Writing in 1887, Ferdinand Tonnies (1957) used the terms to describe the changes in values and orientations that were taking place in life as we moved first from a hunting and gathering society, then to an agricultural society, and then on to an industrial society. Each of these transformations resulted in a shift away from *gemeinschaft* and toward *gesellschaft*, away from a vision of life as sacred community and toward a more secular society. Though *gemeinschaft* and *gesellschaft* do not exist in pure form in the real world, they represent two "ideal types"—two different ways of thinking and living, two different types of cultures, two alternative visions of life.

Tonnies argued that as society moves toward the *gesellschaft* end of the continuum, community values are replaced by contractual ones. Among any collection of people, social relationships don't just happen, they are willed. Individuals decide to associate with each other. The reasons why they decide to associate are important. In *gemeinschaft*, natural will is the motivating force. Individuals decide to relate to each other because doing so has its own intrinsic meaning and significance. There is no tangible goal or benefit in mind for any of the parties to the relationship. In *gesellschaft*, rational will is the motivating force. Individuals decide to relate to each other to reach some goal, to gain some benefit. Without this benefit there would be no relationship. Once the benefit is lost, the relationship ends. In the first instance, the ties among people are moral. In the second instance the ties among people are calculated.

The modern corporation is an example of *gesellschaft*. Within the corporation, relationships are formal and distant, having been prescribed by roles and expectations. Circumstances are evaluated by universal criteria as embodied in policies, rules and protocols. Acceptance is conditional. The more a person cooperates with the corporation and achieves for the corporation, the more likely she or he will be accepted. Relationships are competitive. Those who achieve more are valued more by the corporation. Not all concerns of members are legitimate. Legitimate concerns are bounded by roles rather than needs. Subjectivity is frowned upon. Rationality is prized. Self-interest prevails.

Gesellschaft values make sense in the corporation, and in other organizations such as the army, the research university, and the hospital. But applying the same values to a small African-American church, a family, a social club, a neighborhood, a mutual aid society, a small town, a volunteer social action group, or a school, however, raises important questions of effectiveness and goodness.

All social enterprises must solve the connections problem if they are to function effectively. Members must be sufficiently connected to each other in some way to be able to communicate with each other, understand each other, and coordinate their activities. And members must be sufficiently connected to the enterprise's purposes and values so that, either willingly or unwillingly, they will function to reflect or achieve them.

Gesellschaft enterprises maintain connections by bartering rewards or punishments for loyalty and compliance. Members work for pay or for psychological rewards, and their involvement, as a result, is calculated. As long as they get what they want, they give what they must. But when they calculate otherwise, their involvement decreases.

Gemeinschaft enterprises, by contrast, strive to go beyond calculated to committed involvement. They do not ignore "what gets rewarded gets done," but they also strive to develop relationships among people that have moral overtones. They understand the importance of identifying with place and space over a period of time, and providing members with security, sense, and meaning. And they recognize that in the end the ties that bind us together come from sharing with others a common commitment to a set of ideas and ideals.

Tonnies refers to these ties as community by relationships, community of place, and community of mind. Community by relationships characterizes the special kinds of connections among people that create a unity of being similar to that found in families and other closely knit collections of people. Community of place characterizes the sharing of a common habitat or locale. This sharing of place with others for sustained periods of time creates a special identity and a shared sense of belonging that connects people together in special ways. Community of mind emerges from the binding of people to common goals, shared values, and shared conceptions of being and doing. Together the three represent webs of meaning that connect people together uniquely by creating a special sense of belonging and a strong common identity.

As schools struggle to become communities, they address questions such as the following: What can be done to increase the sense of family, neighborliness, and collegiality among the faculty of a school? How can the faculty become more of a professional community where everyone cares about each other and helps each other to be, to learn together, and to lead together? What kinds of school-parent relationships need to be cultivated to include parents in this emerging community? How can the web of relationships that exist among teachers and between teachers and students be defined so that they embody community? How can teaching and learning settings be arranged so that they are more family-like? How can the school itself, as a collection of families, be more like a neighborhood? What are the shared values and commitments that enable the school to become a community of mind? How will these values and commitments become practical standards that can guide the lives community members want to lead, what community members learn and how, and how community members treat each other? What are the patterns of mutual obligations and duties that emerge in the school as community is achieved?

Though not cast in stone, community understandings have enduring qualities. They are resilient enough to survive the passage of members through the community over time. They are taught to new members, celebrated in customs and rituals, and embodied as standards that govern life in the community. As suggested by Bellah and his colleagues (1985), enduring understandings create a fourth form of community—community of memory. In time, communities of relationships, of place, and of mind become communities of memory. Being a part of a community of memory sustains us when the going is tough, connects us when we are not physically present, and provides us with a history for creating sense and meaning.

Personal Experiences with Community

Let us put our Theory of Community to a test. If we were to share our personal experiences with community, would common themes emerge among them? If so, would our stories and themes fit the *gemeinschaft-gesellschaft* theoretical framework? Would, for example, our stories reveal strong connections themed to communities of relationship, of place, of mind, and of memory? Would our stories provide images of us along with others being transformed from a loose connection of individuals to a "we"? Would moral purposes and moral obligation emerge as important ties for creating this "we," and for governing how we live together and work together? Would new principals of leadership and management emerge? Let us find out.

Take a moment to recall occasions in your personal life when you experienced community. Select one of those occasions that was particularly meaningful to you. Write a story about that occasion that focuses on you as a character, your relationships with others, the events that unfolded, your motivation and that of others, and how you felt being part of this experience. Use your story to make a list of more general characteristics that describes the community you experienced.

I recently asked a group of principals of Jewish schools in the greater Philadelphia area, and a group of Wisconsin and Illinois public school principals who were attending a Principals' Center Institute at Milwaukee's Cardinal Stritch College, to recall their personal experiences with community, write community stories, and then share their stories looking for common themes. The stories here are not meant to tell "the whole story," but to serve as prompts for group discussion. Over a hundred stories emerged. Three of them appear below:

> When I was in high school, a friend's barn burned down. The following weekend, I went with a special group of friends to help with the clean-up. We worked very hard in the heat and the dirt. We shovelled ashes, lifted burned beams, tended cattle, shovelled straw, and generally did things that I wouldn't have done if told to. But voluntarily, I worked all weekend with friends, and *loved it*. We felt that we had done something important for someone we cared

about. I loved that weekend—doing something wonderful, something important, something worth doing, and doing it with others.

When I think of community, I think of my long term association with Alcoholics Anonymous—an association where I feel cared for no matter how well I think I'm doing. When I first joined, I found myself embraced by others, and felt totally accepted and understood. I felt I could count on them at any time of the day or night, and that they could count on me. All of us were just a phone call away from each other. When we are together we really listen to each other, and care about each other. We feel responsible for each other. Belonging is voluntary, and the love we get and give is unconditional. People may challenge me, but because they care about what's good *for me*. Membership is simple (a willingness to get and give help) and all structure is *only* used to support the goal of recovering for all those in the group. Also, we all share a common experience that we survived, and all believe that we need help. There is real interdependence.

A caring community that I experienced was teaching in a grade 7–8 language-arts/social studies team of five teachers in a small K–12 district. We were a pilot IGE (Individually Guided Education) junior high in the early seventies. The team was made up of two veteran teachers, and three novice teachers. We shared a commitment to work together and teach together in ways that resulted in student learning. So, we were constantly evaluating everything, and students were a big part of that evaluation. We were constantly engaged in learning more, and in adjusting our practice. We had total control over the teaching and learning environment. We worked very visibly in front of each other—as if we were one class with five teachers rather than a collection of five teachers and five classes. We worked hard. We knew what we wanted to accomplish, and we believed in what we were doing. We felt special. We all had different talents, and we were better because of that. We were better because of each other. We were professionally close rather than personally close. We had high expectations for what we wanted to do, and for each other, and we worked hard to get the job done.

After the stories were written, and shared in small groups, each group reported to the group as a whole. The characteristics of community that were shared were written on flip charts for discussion and later use. Below are the characteristics from both the Philadelphia-area and the Wisconsin/Illinois principals:

purpose
focus
commitment to purpose
stayed focused on purpose and goals
rallied around a struggle
rolled up our sleeves and pitched in
we went beyond the call of duty
passion, spirit
feeling of spirituality about the goals
we coordinated informally
we made decisions easily
manageable size
trust
free to take risks
we know each other well
there for each other
respect for each other
committed to each other
free to try new things
everyone is involved
everyone is needed
protective of each other
unconditional acceptance, belonging
safe-haven
respect for individual differences
shared emotion shared celebrations
shared hurts shared workload
shared responsibility
self-managing as individuals and group

everyone feels personally responsible for success

everybody feels obligated to do the right thing

less dependent on a leader and more on ourselves

people depend on each other, are there for each other

everyone has something valuable to contribute

fight fair—not win/lose but problem solving

frequent dialogue, open communication

choice, involvement is voluntary

From this list it becomes clear that thinking about schools as moral communities, and struggling to transform them in this direction, provides the kind of focus on goals, commitment to shared purpose and values, connections among people, and moral authority for getting things done that raises serious challenges to our existing theories of management and leadership.

What are the implications of community for how we understand schools and how we arrange for teaching and learning? With community as the theory, we would have to restructure in such a way that the school itself is not defined by brick and mortar but by ideas and by tight connections. Creating communities of relationships and of place, for example, might well mean changing most high schools from large organizations into several small schools— rarely exceeding 400 or so students. The importance of creating sustained relationships would require that students and teachers stay together for longer periods of time. Teaching in fifty-minute episodes would have to be replaced with something else. Elementary schools would have to give serious consideration to organizing themselves into smaller and probably multi-aged families. Discipline problems would no longer be resolved on psychological principles but on moral ones. The use of moral principles would require schools to abandon such taken-for-granted ideas as having explicit rules linked to clearly stated consequences that are uniformly applied. Instead, we would have to develop social contracts, constitutions, and normative codes. Inservice education and staff development would move from the administrative side of the ledger to the teacher side as part of teachers' ongoing commitment to practice at the edge of their craft. Extrinsic reward systems

would have to disappear. The number of specialists would probably be reduced and pull-outs would be less common as "families"
composed of teachers and students, like traditional families composed of parents and children, began to take fuller responsibility
for solving their own problems. And all of these changes would
necessitate the invention of new standards of quality, new strategies for accountability, and new ways of working with people—the
invention of a new educational administration, in other words.

Why should we develop a new educational administration—
one embedded in a Theory of Community? Because *gesellschaft* theories of schooling are not able to provide the kind of connections
we now need in schools for them to be effective in today's world.
Carla Nuxoll (1994), a high school teacher from Spokane, Washington, puts the problem this way:

> What happens when the sense of belonging . . . is missing from the
> school? What happens if the adults in the school *never* talk about
> higher purposes or mission or meaning in any intentional way with
> each other or with the students? What if teachers and students *never*
> talk about what they are trying to achieve together? What is the
> likely result of this lack of shared purpose?
>
> We unintentionally create a dysfunctional, but not an atypical
> school. I believe many schools skip over community building, i.e.,
> creating a shared purpose, to get on with the practical and time-
> devouring busy-ness of school—classes, subject-matter, discipline,
> scheduling, grading, and paperwork. As adults, we can still func-
> tion—though not joyfully—within such a setting. We rely on our
> individual, and often purely private understanding of mission to
> see past the routine to the ideals we strive to achieve. Our students,
> however, sense our fragmentation and lack of unity and purpose.
> They have neither the maturity nor the experience to deal with the
> conflicting purposes and expectations which swirl around them.
> Many times they feel lost and overwhelmed. School for them is not
> safe and secure, but arbitrary and pointless, run by adults all on a
> game plan that they are not allowed to understand.

Nuxoll invited several high school students to share "a couple
of ideas for changing education." She sums up their responses as
follows:

Please listen to our plea. We are lonely, disaffected, confused, and "lost all the time in schooling," yet we are yearning for challenge and genuine success. I hear them beg the adults who are supposed to know to help them find a purpose and meaning in their schooling beyond tomorrow's test, and even beyond tomorrow's career. But how do we help them uncover purpose? I believe it means having real conversations with them about each other, and about commitments and values, about caring and striving. It means discussing ideals, and revealing the searching, reflecting, and struggling which we know is the human condition. It means getting our act together in schools to articulate and model the value of excellence for its own sake. It means showing we care for one another, and that each student is known and respected. It means hard work, creating this community of learners, but work of the noblest kind.

Restoring Character to School Leadership

Changing our theory from school-as-organization to school-as-moral-community is the way to restore integrity and character to the literature on school organization, management, and leadership. Organizations become communities when they are "infused with value," to use Selznick's term (1957). This infusion provides a distinct identity composed of "distinctive outlook, habits, and other commitments [that] are unified, coloring all aspects of organizational life and lending it a *social integration* that goes well beyond formal organization and command" (p. 40).

Understanding schools as moral communities requires the development of a distinct leadership for the schoolhouse. Key to this leadership would be the cultivation of moral authority as the basis for what people do. Moral authority comes from the development of shared agreements and compacts that bring community members together into a shared followership. Moral authority allows the school as community to speak to teachers, students, and parents as a moral voice. Moral communities are convenantal. They take their cue from Jeremiah (31:33), which points out that for laws to be effective they must be planted in the heart rather than written on stone—the theme of the next chapter.

Chapter Four

Establishing a Moral Voice

Compacts and shared commitments among principals, parents, teachers, and students, and the moral authority they provide, are key in applying Community Theory to schools. As this authority becomes established, it speaks as a moral voice that substitutes for the usual management systems and leadership strategies we now use to provide direction, and to control people and events. This moral voice compels everyone in the school to meet their commitments, and to become self-managing.

As simple as the idea of moral voice is, it has the potential to revolutionize school leadership. Instead of thinking about bureaucratic management and personal leadership as the driving forces that push and pull the school and its members forward, moral voice helps us think of leadership more as the cultivation of a shared followership. Community members are bonded together as they are bound to share commitments in a covenantal relationship. Principals and other administrators remain important, but are differently important. They have special responsibilities to behave as head followers of the community's ideas, values, and shared commitments.

Community Theory is uniquely suited to schools because schools lend themselves to the cultivation of moral voice. By contrast, it is hard to think about moral authority as the prime basis for what people think and do in corporations and other *gesellschaft* organizations. Sure, workers bring moral voices with them from home, church, and other places. And sure, all work has moral overtones. There is, for example, dignity in doing one's best whatever the task. People should give a fair day's work for a fair day's pay. Many corporations make products and provide services that uplift the human condition. And many employees become committed to and inspired by corporate goals, deriving deep satisfaction from their accomplishments on behalf of these goals as a result. But much of this good feeling is synthetic, having been created by charismatic leadership and clever management strategies rather than having been inspired by the nature of the work itself.

By and large, corporations and other *gesellschaft* employers offer people jobs, and then rely on exchanging material benefits and psychological need-fulfillment for the work that people do. At root, the ties that hold everything together are calculated. Given these conditions, the use of management systems accompanied by attention to human relations, as in the High Performance Theory, is both a wise and effective way to ensure quality products and services, as well as efficient worker performance.

Schools and other *gemeinschaft* enterprises, however, are different. Schools have joblike dimensions, but are capable of transcending these dimensions morally by calling principals, parents, teachers, and students to serve ideas and ideals that are considered to be virtuous. To be called to serve is to be motivated by inner urges, by feelings of obligation and commitment, and by norms that speak as a moral voice. If a secret exists that accounts for the power of community, it is the moral voice that community provides. Etzioni (1993) explains,

> When the term *community* is used, the first notion that typically comes to mind is a place in which people know and care for one another—the kind of place in which people do not merely ask 'How are you?' as a formality, but care about the answer. This weness . . . is indeed part of its essence. Our focus here, though, is on another element of community, crucial for the issues at hand: *Communities speak to us in moral voices. They lay claims on their members. Indeed, they are the most important sustaining source of moral voices other than the inner self* [p. 31].

Though recognizing the importance of self-interest and individual choice as driving forces, and the power of satisfying individual needs as sources of motivation, Etzioni argues for a broader norm-referenced view of human nature. He believes "individuals . . . [are] able to act rationally and on their own, advancing their self or 'I,' but their ability to do so is deeply affected by how well they are anchored within a sound community, and sustained by firm moral and emotive personal underpinning—a community they perceive as theirs, as a 'We,' rather than as an imposed, restraining 'They'" (Etzioni, 1988 p. ix–x). To him, it is morality, emotions, and social bonds in the form of what we believe, how we feel, and the norms and cultural meanings we share with important others that count the most as we decide how to lead our lives.

In sum, a *gesellschaft* theory of schools as organizations assumes that individuals make independent decisions by calculating costs and benefits of various alternatives as they seek to maximize their gains and cut their losses. Community Theory, on the other hand, recognizes that humans are norm-referenced decision makers. They take into account the norms and shared realities of others whose identities are important to them, and they seek not only to advance their own interests, but those of the group. They accept the reality that sometimes the former has to be sacrificed for the latter. When norms come from values and beliefs that are shared, and when group identities are freely chosen, the norms speak as a compelling moral voice. They provide guidance and affirm the decisions one makes. In effect, moral voice becomes a substitute for the kind of leadership advocated in *gesellschaft* organizations, and encourages people to become self-managing.

Why is the moral voice of community so important in today's schools? Indeed, why is the moral voice of community so important in today's world? Because without it, we respond to other voices—voices that acknowledge norms that might be questionable, harmful, or even personally destructive. Students are particularly vulnerable. They can respond to the moral voice of school as community. In the absence of this voice, they can respond to the norms of a separate—and often dysfunctional—student subculture. But respond they must, for it is part of our human nature to be norm-referenced. This is the way we know we belong. This is the way we secure our personal identities. And this is the way we find sense and meaning in our lives.

Student subcultures have always been alive and well in schools, dictating patterns of dress, speech habits, and fairly harmless rites and rituals of passage from childhood through adolescence to adulthood. But in many of today's schools, the gap between the student subculture and the culture of the school itself has never been greater. Adults have never counted for less in the lives of the students they are supposed to be serving. And students are forced to turn more and more to themselves to get their needs met, to find connections, to belong, to find meaning.

As the grip of the student subculture tightens, norms that were once harmless can be replaced by norms that are harmful and often destructive. Student study habits, sexual habits, modes of interaction with adults, forms of amusement, and other standards of beliefs and behaviors can be negatively affected as a result. Could this be why over 80 percent of the students who participated in the twenty-fourth annual survey of High Achievers (Associated Press, 1993) admitted to routinely cheating, and seeing nothing wrong with this behavior? These were students who were elected to *Who's Who Among American High School Students* in 1992–93. Could this be why roughly two-thirds of the students surveyed in 1992 by the Institute for Ethics (Parker, 1994) said they cheated on an exam at least once during that year? About 39 percent of the boys and 26 percent of the girls surveyed also admitted to shoplifting at least once, too. Could this be why some students study less than they normally might want to, and perform less ably in school than they can? Could this be why it is common for some students to witness others spray-painting the walls of the school, or to witness others hurling racial epithets or other insults at students who are different, and to do nothing about it?

A decade ago I would have been inclined to describe the events that follow as a worst-case scenario. But in today's schools, such events are becoming a common occurrence. A recent newspaper article (Fox, 1994) reported that a teenage gunman had killed a four-year-old boy in a drive-by shooting. The assailant was a model student in grade school, but "gave in to peer pressure of gangs in middle school." One teacher who knew the youngster commented, "After the kids leave the elementary school, and go to the middle school, it's typical that they give in to peer pressure and join gangs." She stated, "I put this student at the top of the list when it came to good kids." She meant, of course, that that was until the student subculture captured his mind, his heart, and then his behavior.

Norms work similarly at home. Many youngsters wish that their parents would provide a standard of behavior for them—one that gives them a "face-saving" out to resist the norms of peers. A youngster can say no to peer pressure and still belong if she or he has an acceptable excuse such as, "My folks will just kill me if I do that!" Some teasing will surely follow (accompanied by a lot of envy) but the group will understand. Unfortunately, too many youngsters don't have acceptable excuses, and thus are required to bend to peer pressure as the price for belonging, no matter what the consequences.

U.S. and Canadian teachers tell me that by grade 3 students are already shifting more into the student subculture, and by grade 5 they are pretty much driven by the norms of this group rather than the norms of the school at large. And yet it doesn't have to be this way. As long as we continue to ignore the importance of cultivating norms and cultures that can speak to us as moral voices, students will continue to turn to themselves, and to the norms they create for themselves to get their own needs met. The moral voice of community can help to "domesticate" these haphazard and dangerous norms by providing students with a choice—a safe alternative to what they now have on their own. But what about the negative side of developing norm systems? Isn't it true that norm systems put pressure on people to conform, to give up their personal identities? In the end, doesn't Community Theory squash individual rights and freedoms, and dim initiative? In a democratic society such as we share in Canada and the United States, the rights of individuals must be protected. To do otherwise is to create an authoritarian rather than authoritative community. To Aristotle, it was not so much unity but harmony that defined a community. Some things are shared. Other things are not. But the blending of the two is harmonious. And this harmony of distinct but complementary ideas and personalities is held together by the special quality of relationships that exist in communities.

In *Nichomachean Ethics*, Aristotle referred to this special quality of relationships as "friendship." Today, friendship is defined interpersonally as people liking or enjoying one another. But in its traditional sense, friendship was known by two other essential elements. Friends must be helpful to one another. And friends must share a common commitment to the good (Bellah and others, 1985, p. 115). Key in Community Theory is the idea that the core of what friendship is, and the core of why it sustains itself, is the presence of common moral commitments. In schools as communities, Aristotle's ideas about friendship can be applied to teachers, and parallel the concept of colleagueship that comes from mutual respect, common traditions, and a commitment to help one another. When we apply Aristotle's ideas about friendship to teachers and students, we speak to teachers not as being friends in a peer sense, but as being friends for having accepted their roles to act morally *in loco parentis*.

Forging Agreements

What should be the content of the school's core of shared values, ideas, and purposes? In the end this question must be addressed by the teachers, parents, and students of each individual school as it struggles to become a community. The unique characteristics of schools as communities, however, require that certain common issues be addressed. Schools, for example, should strive to become purposeful communities, caring communities, inquiring communities, and respectful communities that are able to function successfully in a democratic society. Thus school covenants need to be concerned with such questions as:

What do we want students to know?

What do we want students to become?

How do we want them to think?

How do we want them to reason?

What do we want them to value and believe?

How can we help them become persons of character in our democratic society?

How do we want them to live their lives together in this school, to care for each other, to help each other, to respect each other?

How do we want them to work together, to inquire together, to learn together.

What do we believe about how students learn?

How should we think about our roles as teachers, counselors, and friends?

What are our responsibilities as we stand *in loco parentis* to our students?

How will we work together as adults?

What will our obligations be to each other?

How will we share the burdens of leadership in this school?

What do we believe about accountability?

Where do parents fit into the picture?

What obligations and commitments should we make to parents and what obligations and commitments should we expect from them?

Different schools will answer these questions differently, and this raises still another question. Does anything go, or are some answers to these questions better than others? Some answers *are* better than others, but which answers are better depends upon whether the theory for the school is community or something else. Thus while communities need not look exactly alike, and while not everyone needs to believe in exactly the same things, there are boundaries of differences that cannot be crossed. Community brings to all schools a unique definition, a unique value system, and a unique way of life.

For example, consider the question, What do we believe about how students learn? Following Saphier and D'Auria's ideas (1993, p. 15), imagine two schools that answer the question of student learning differently. One school espouses "Life-Liberating" beliefs, and the other "Life-Limiting" beliefs contrasted as follows:

All children are capable of high achievement, not just the fastest and most competent.	*versus*	Only the few bright can achieve at a high level.
You're not supposed to understand everything the first time around.	*versus*	Speed is what counts. Faster is smarter.
Consistent effort is the main determinant of success.	*versus*	Inborn intelligence is the main determinant of success.
Mistakes help one learn.	*versus*	Mistakes are a sign of weakness.

	versus	
Good students work together, and solicit help from one another.		Competition is necessary to bring out the best in our students.

Given these different beliefs about student learning, we can expect each of the schools to develop quite different sets of curriculum and teaching and evaluation policies, and quite different ways of operating. But which view is better? Saphier and D'Auria provide compelling arguments for choosing the "Life-Liberating" beliefs over the "Life-Limiting" beliefs. They point out, for example, that by age three nearly all children in the United States have mastered perhaps the most complex task with which they will ever be confronted—the English language. This reality, they argue, should be proof enough for the belief that all children are capable of high achievement. Convincing arguments continue for the other beliefs about learning as well. But if Community Theory is the right choice for schools, the "Life-Liberating" beliefs must be chosen not just because they can be logically argued, but because they are consistent with the values of community.

Beliefs about learning have a lot to do with beliefs about relationships. Community Theory provides us with an exacting standard for thinking about relationships among students, between teachers and students, and among teachers. This standard is different from the one that characterizes more *gesellschaft* organizations (see "Relationships in Communities," Chapter 3 of Sergiovanni, 1994). Teachers, for example, will have to decide: Will relationships with students be like those of a professional expert who treats students like clients? Or will relationships be more like those of a parent who treats students like family members? Will students be given equal treatment in accordance with uniform standards, rules, and regulations? Or will students be treated more preferentially and individually? Will role relationships and job descriptions narrowly define specific topics for attention and discussion with students? Or will relationships be considered unbounded by roles, and thus more inclusive and holistic? Will students have to earn the right to be regarded as "good" and to maintain their standing in the school? Or will students be accepted completely simply because they have enrolled in the school? Do we decide that a certain distance needs to be maintained between teachers and students in order for professional interests and concerns to remain uncompromised? Or do we view ourselves as part of a teacher-student "we" that compels us to work closely with students in identifying common interests, concerns, and standards for decision making? Will good relationships be sought with students in order to motivate them to learn more? Or will good relationships be viewed as ends worthy in and of themselves?

The sociologist Talcott Parsons (1951) argues that communities are defined by the pattern of relationships that is represented by the first alternative in each of the paired statements above. This pattern values subjectivity, effectiveness, collective orientation, particularism, human fallibility, renewal, efficacy, and other human characteristics that point to the "Life-Liberating" beliefs about teaching and learning.

In *Moral Leadership* (1992), I pointed out that when shared purposes and the social contracts they imply become the prime source of authority for what happens in the school, the school itself becomes a covenantal community. The choice of the word *covenantal* was deliberate; its use implies that the school changes from a secular to a sacred enterprise, from a mere instrument designed to achieve certain ends to a virtuous enterprise.

A covenantal community is a group of people who share certain purposes, values, and beliefs, who feel a strong sense of place, and who think of the welfare of the group as being more important than that of the individual. This community inspires deep loyalty, and compels members to work together for the common good (pp. 102–103).

Covenant is a sacred metaphor with biblical roots. Genesis, as Pohly (1993) points out, speaks to God's covenant with Israel as a reciprocal agreement of solemn promises and expected responses as follows: "I will make you a great nation . . . " (Gen. 12:2), and in return, "you shall keep my covenant . . . " (Gen. 17:9). In covenantal communities, leaders must not only help bring about a shared consensus of ideas, model these ideas, and then help others to embody them in their daily lives, but they must bring together a shared commitment among members to maintain accountability for living the covenant.

In a sense, this covenant sounds like a contract that specifies mutual obligations, and exacts penalties for any party to the contract who doesn't meet her or his commitments. But covenants are more than contracts. Contracts refer to bottom lines and minimums. Covenants, by contrast, refer to top lines and maximums. As Max De Pree, a well-known corporate executive who understands the difference between *gesellschaft* and *gemeinschaft* enterprises, puts it: "Contracts are a small part of our relationship. A complete relationship needs a covenant. . . . A covenantal relationship rests on a shared commitment to ideas, to issues, to values, to goals. . . . Covenantal relationships reflect unity, and grace, and poise. They are expressions of the sacred nature of the relationships" (1989, p. 12).

One of the first things Peter Hutchinson did when he became the Minneapolis school superintendent was to seek a voluntary personal commitment from students, families, teachers, school staff, administrators, the school board, and community members to a common set of values and expectations. Hutchinson decided to use the term *covenant* over promise or pledge because he wanted those who committed themselves to do more than promise individually to meet their commitments. He wanted them to help each other achieve the common purpose of making the Minneapolis schools better. To Hutchinson this covenant "is a voluntary *re-commitment* for all of us. It signals to the community that we are all in this together, and shows how dependent we are on each other to provide a good education for all students" (Panasonic Foundation, 1994).

Those who choose to re-commit are asked to sign "The Minneapolis Covenant," a statement of personal responsibility and accountability. To date, over 27,000 covenants have been signed. Each one has been personally countersigned by Hutchinson. "I spent *many* evenings signing the covenants, and I was continually impressed with the thoughtfulness of student responses. It made me very aware of how much our students, their families, and our teachers care about success. I was also very interested in the array of community signers—from school volunteers, to business people, to neighbors and friends. Minneapolis is clearly a community that cares about kids" (Minneapolis Public Schools, 1994). The covenant appears as Exhibit 4.1.

At their best, covenants involve everyone who has a stake in the welfare of the school. They imply not only a commitment of personal responsibility, but a commitment of shared responsibility. But forging a common commitment from across the wide spectrum of

Exhibit 4.1. The Minneapolis Covenant.

EDUCATION TAKES EVERYONE

The Minneapolis Covenant

COVENANT *1. a formal, solemn and binding agreement. 2. a written agreement or promise usually between two or more parties, especially for the performance of some action. It is a declaration of intent by all parties who sign to help each other achieve mutual objectives.*

These promises are voluntary commitments made by individuals to themselves and to others.

As a student. . .

I promise to. . .
★ attend school regularly
★ work hard to do my best in class and schoolwork
★ help to keep my school safe
★ ask for help when I need it
★ respect and cooperate with other students and adults

My personal promise:

_____

_____
school   home room

I need. . .
★ teachers and school staff who care about me
★ people who believe I can learn
★ schools that are safe
★ respect for my culture and me as an individual
★ a family and community that support me
★ time with caring adults

_____
student signature

As a parent / caring adult. . .

I promise to . . .
★ have high expectations for my child as an individual
★ help my child attend school and be on time
★ find a quiet place for schoolwork and make sure work is done
★ help my child learn to resolve conflicts in positive ways
★ communicate and work with teachers and school staff to support and challenge my child
★ respect school staff and the cultural differences of others

I need. . .
★ teachers and support staff who respect my role as a parent/caring adult
★ clear and frequent communication with school
★ respect for my culture, and me and my children as individuals
★ a community that supports families

My personal promise:

_____

_____
parent / caring adult signature

As a staff person. . .
(teacher, support staff or administrator)

I promise to. . .
★ show that I care about all students
★ have high expectations for myself, students and other staff
★ communicate and work with families to support students' learning
★ provide a safe environment for learning
★ respect the cultural differences of students and their families

I need. . .
★ students who are ready and willing to learn
★ respect and support from students, families, other staff and administration
★ assistance from staff and administration in removing barriers which prevent me from doing my best for students
★ respect and support from the community

_____
teacher

_____
teacher

_____
principal

_____
school staff member

As Superintendent. . .

I promise to. . .
★ believe that all students can achieve
★ have challenging expectations for students, families and staff
★ remove barriers to improved performance on all levels
★ promote education and the Minneapolis Public Schools
★ listen, hear and respond to feedback from students, staff and the community
★ tell the truth in love

I need. . .
★ staff, students, families and community committed to education and lifelong learning
★ a staff willing to challenge old assumptions and look for new ways to solve problems
★ a school board that is focused on what students need to achieve
★ students, staff and community members to communicate their needs and listen to one another
★ a community that supports youth and families

Peter Hutchinson, Minneapolis Public Schools Superintendent

As a member of the School Board. . .

I promise to do all I can to meet the needs expressed in this pledge by students, families, staff, superintendent and the community. I will work to the best of my ability to create a school district and community where everyone can keep their covenants with each other.

board member

As a member of the Minneapolis community. . .

I promise to. . .
★ respect, encourage and support students, families and teachers
★ be an active, contributing partner with the schools
★ make Minneapolis a safe and exciting place for students, families and teachers
★ support learning regardless of where it occurs
★ provide jobs and post-high school opportunities

I need. . .
★ educated and responsible workers and fellow citizens
★ an educational system that invites community input and feedback
★ opportunities to be involved in producing educational results

community member   *community member*

community member   *community member*

community member   *community member*

MINNEAPOLIS PUBLIC SCHOOLS
1993 - 1994

Source: Reprinted with permission of the Minneapolis Public Schools.

stakeholders is often difficult. One way to begin the task is by entering into more limited agreements. Exhibit 4.2, for example, provides an agreement in the form of a set of standards that the Rocky Mountain School of Expeditionary Learning expects of its students. This agreement is linked to a set of values and beliefs that school officials feel embodies the purposes and core values of the school itself. Linking expectations to values is critical for otherwise expectations lose moral meaning. When this happens they become little more than lists of *gesellschaft* rules and consequences.

Not only are students expected to sign the agreement, thus pledging personal responsibility for embodying its beliefs, but their parents are expected to sign as well. As the next step, a broader agreement might be struck that includes the obligations of principals, teachers, and board members, as well as students and parents. Such an agreement should make clear to all that for individual obligations to be met, responsibility must not only be personal but collective.

The Basic School

Ernest Boyer and his colleagues at the Carnegie Foundation for the Advancement of Teaching have been at work developing a school renewal model, called the Basic School to reflect its emphasis on educating children from kindergarten through grade 4. The Basic School is built on the conviction that every child has a right to a quality education, that all children can be successful in school, and that schools should be held to high standards. Beyond these beliefs is a theory of schooling that places connections at the center. On the one hand, the Basic School strives to connect parents, principals, teachers, and students together in such a way that they become a caring and industrious community. Being connected in this way means being committed to a common focus and a common set of ideas about how the Basic School works, and what it should accomplish. On the other hand, the Basic School strives to function as a connected institution in which eight basic building blocks fit together making the whole greater than its parts. Both kinds of connections are intended to overcome the fragmentation of purpose and practice that now characterizes our educational system. Boyer describes the eight building blocks as follows:

1. A Community of Learning

Above all else, the Basic School is a community of learning, a purposeful place with a clear and vital mission. Teachers, staff, students and parents have a shared vision of what the school is seeking to accomplish. For this to happen, the school must be kept small, and time set aside for people to work together. All members of the community are empowered to fulfill the school's mission, and it is here that the principal's role is absolutely crucial. It is her or his vision and leadership, supported by committed teachers, that will ensure success.

2. The Centrality of Language

The Basic School views proficiency in language as central to all learning, the means by which all other subjects are pursued. The Basic School is a place where language is defined broadly to include the full range of symbols, including verbal literacy— reading, writing, speaking, listening—as well as numeracy and the arts. All of these tools, while taught separately, are also integrated throughout the entire curriculum.

3. A Coherent Curriculum

In the Basic School, all students will become well informed in the core subjects—science, history, geography, civics, literature, health, and other essential fields. But rather than focus on isolated subjects, the Basic School has a core curriculum framework designed to promote both comprehensiveness and coherence so that the core subjects are used to illuminate eight essential themes. These themes, called the "Human Commonalities," embrace experiences shared by all people, integrate knowledge across the disciplines, relate the curriculum to the lives of students, and help children understand not only their own heritage, but the traditions of other cultures.

4. Empowered Students

In the Basic School, students are empowered in a climate of active learning where they learn to be creative rather than competitive. Children are grouped in different ways to achieve different ends— administrative, pedagogical, and social—and move easily from one arrangement to another.

Exhibit 4.2. Rocky Mountain School of Expeditionary Learning Program Participation Agreement.

Student Agreement for Participation in the Rocky Mountain School of Expeditionary Learning Program

I, _____ , understand that the Rocky Mountain School of Expeditionary Learning has been founded and is directed by ten specific principles of design. In accordance with these principles, the following is a list of expectations for my behavior and performance at RMSEL that constitutes a contractual agreement between myself and the school.

As a student of RMSEL, I am committed to the following:

The Primacy of Self Discovery

I am excited about the prospect of discovering my abilities, values, and "grand passions" and am committed to providing the perseverance, fitness, craftsmanship, imagination, self-discipline, and significant achievement necessary to do so.

The Having of Wonderful Ideas

I agree to share my ideas with classmates, teachers, and other RMSEL community members whenever appropriate and in turn, I agree to respect the ideas and suggestions of classmates, teachers, and RMSEL community members that are shared with me.

The Responsibility of Learning

With the help of my teachers, parents, and other mentors, I agree to take on more responsibility for directing my own personal learning and, as appropriate, that of my RMSEL community.

Intimacy and Caring

I promise to conduct myself in such a way as to be considered a trustworthy, reliable, concerned, caring, and respected member of the RMSEL community. I will act in accordance with the RMSEL Code of Conduct. I will consider myself a role model for other students in the school and as such, I agree to work with younger students to assist them in their development and education as appropriate.

Success and Failure

I am committed to achieving academic success. I will work hard, take risks, and overcome challenges. In the event some of my efforts fail, I promise to work hard to prevail against adversity and to learn to turn the disabilities I face into opportunities.

Collaboration and Competition

I am committed to academic and character achievement that exceeds what I would describe as my own personal best. I promise to persistently work towards achieving rigorous standards of academic and character excellence as prescribed by the school even if that means I perform a task over and over and over until I attain this goal. In addition, I promise to be a productive member of any group with which I work.

Diversity and Inclusivity

I will learn more about my own personal history and culture as well as the histories and cultures of my fellow RMSEL community members and will demonstrate nothing but the highest respect for people of all walks of life in everything I do.

The Natural World

I will respect the natural world and commit to taking responsibility for caring for the environment.

Solitude and Reflection

I will use time for solitude and reflection productively to explore my thoughts and to create ideas that I will exchange with other students and with adults.

Service and Compassion

I believe that we are crew and not passengers in life. I will demonstrate this belief by participating in service projects so that I can learn from and be of service to others.

I have read and understand the list of expectations and agree to participate in the RMSEL program in accordance with these expectations. I understand that failure to do so will result in counseling sessions with my teacher(s) and my parents(s) and will impact my evaluations at RMSEL.

_____   _____

Student Signature   Date

_____   _____

Parent Signature   Date

Parental Commitment to this Agreement

As parent of this RMSEL student, I agree to assist my child in maintaining the level of participation outlined in the Student Contract and agree to support the staff and school in this effort. In addition, I agree to:

- support the pursuit of education in my home.
- see to it that my child attends school every day except in the case of illness or emergency.
- participate in two to four parent/teacher conferences a year.
- volunteer to assist the school in whatever way is practical for me.

I understand that the students of RMSEL are subject to its Code of Conduct and that the school operates strictly in accordance with Colorado State Law regarding student behavior.

_____   _____

Signature   Date

Source: Reprinted with permission of the Rocky Mountain School of Expeditionary Learning.

Ideally, the Basic School has rich resources for learning—good books, magazines and up-to-date reference materials, as well as videocassettes, compact discs, computer software, audio equipment, and telecommunication capabilities. Every classroom is electronically connected to a central learning center.

The Basic School has outdoor space for play and organized games, and a garden maintained by students. The school also views the surrounding community as a resource, and students visit local libraries, zoos, and supermarkets to enrich their learning.

5. Teachers as Leaders

Teachers are leaders in the Basic School, and the principal is head teacher. The teachers are well informed, able to relate their knowledge to the readiness of their students, and trusted by children and adults. They genuinely like children and they work well with other educators and parents.

Basic School teachers are organized into horizontal grade-level teams and vertical K-4 "family" teams. They are continually renewed through university-sponsored courses, inservice mentoring, and coaching. They also have study leaves to engage in research and to continue their education.

6. Parents as Partners

Parents are a child's first and most essential teachers, and in the Basic School they are also active and committed members of the learning community. The school establishes an early partnership with parents through a preschool PTA. Every parent enrolling a child in the Basic School enters into a learning covenant which clearly defines the school's goals and expected outcomes. Parents, in turn, pledge to do all they can to assist their child's learning.

The Basic School has an ongoing parent consultation schedule in which teachers report to parents on school and student progress in achieving objectives. Parents are also involved in a wide range of school activities based on their response to a parent interest inventory that is filled out at the beginning of the year. A parent coordinator maintains close communication with parents throughout the year, and the school has set aside a place where parents can get together and chat informally over coffee with each other and with teachers.

7. Services for Children

The Basic School goes beyond the academic to focus on the whole child. A nurse or other health professional is available to provide screening procedures, primary care where appropriate, and emergency care. The school offers a counseling service to provide emotional and social support for children. It also has a collaborative relationship with both public and private health and social service agencies in the community, and makes referrals as needed for students and families.

Responding to changes in family life, the Basic School offers an optional before- and after-school enrichment program, paid for through parent fees or public funds for families in need of support. The school may also offer an optional Saturday school and summer enrichment program.

8. Measuring for Success

Finally, the Basic School maintains high academic standards by carefully and continuously evaluating each student's progress. Reading, math, and the arts are assessed separately to ensure that all students become proficient in the basic tools of learning. Teachers asses general knowledge through a program embedded in the curriculum. The school rejects early standardized evaluation, and state or national assessment is done only in the fourth grade [Boyer, 1994, pp. 30–32].

The curriculum of the Basic School revolves around eight themes referred to as the "Human Commonalities"—again reflecting connections (Boyer, 1994). This time the connections are among the disciplines, and the perennial problems humans face as they struggle to live vital and productive lives individually, socially, economically, and democratically. The commonalities include *the life-cycle,* which enables students to understand the processes of life from birth through growth and life to death. Subjects that support this theme are biology, hygiene, health, and nutrition. Next is *the use of symbols,* which enables students to understand that people are connected to each other through such essential systems as verbal literacy, mathematical literacy, and aesthetic literacy. The subjects that support this theme are the study of language, mathematics, and arts. Third is *response to the aesthetic,* which enables students to explore the use of arts to express ideas and feelings, and to appreciate how the visual and performing arts have evolved in different cultures. The subjects that support this theme are music, dance, theater, and the visual arts. Fourth is *a sense of time,* which enables students to understand their own place in the world by recalling the past, exploring roots, and anticipating the future. The subject area that supports this theme is history. Fifth is *groups and institutions,* which enables students to understand that everyone holds membership in groups as they seek to belong, to secure their own personal identities, and to serve the common good. Beginning with the family, the nature of institutions as the social fabric of human existence is explored, with the intent to develop civic and social responsibility. The subjects that support this theme are civics and social studies. Sixth is *producing and consuming,* which enables students to learn that all people engage in making useful things, and that patterns of production and consumption provide a source of energy for the development of society and for the well-being of its members. This theme involves such subjects as economics, career planning, and vocational studies. Seventh is *connecting to nature,* which enables students to recognize that all forms of life are connected, and to understand the scientific aspects of our natural world. The subjects that support this theme are science, geography, astronomy, technology, and environmental studies. And the final theme is *living with purpose,* which enables students to understand the human search for meaning in life, the importance of values and ethics, and the roles that spirituality and religion play in the human experience. This theme invites the study of world religion, values, and ethics.

The Basic School provides a common curriculum that emphasizes connections among the disciplines and their connections to life, a common focus of purpose and ideals that emphasizes connections of the mind and heart, and a common set of building blocks that emphasizes connections among various school dimensions. Common connections help the school become a community of mind. Commitment to common connections allows the school to speak with a moral voice.

Schools with Character

In 1990, the Rand Corporation published *High Schools with Character* (Hill, Foster, and Gendler, 1990), which reported results from a study of thirteen Catholic, special-purpose public, and comprehensive public high schools serving similar populations of students in New York City and Washington, D.C. The researchers found more similarity in characteristics and performance among the Catholic and special-purpose public schools than differences, but dramatic differences between both of them and the comprehensive public schools. They refer to the first group as "focused" and the second group as "zoned" schools.

Students in the focused schools graduated at a much higher rate than those in the zoned schools. Only 30 percent of students in the zoned schools took the SAT test, as compared with 82 percent of students in focused Catholic and 66 percent of students in focused public schools, and zoned-school student scores were well below the scores of focused-school students.

Responding to a 52-item survey, focused-school students reported higher levels of school pride, a better atmosphere for learning, and felt their schools were in better condition. Table 4.1 presents examples of the items along with mean scores that compare zoned-school students' responses with focused-school students' responses. Students responded on a 1–5 scale (1 equals almost never to 5 equals almost always). Note that focused-school students had higher mean scores (significant at the .001 level) on all the items shown that reflected well on their schools.

A key difference between focused and zoned schools was the ability of the former to speak to principals, parents, teachers, and students in a moral voice that compelled them to pull together in a common cause, and to accept their share of personal and communal responsibility for ensuring that commitments to the common cause were met. Focused schools, in other words, were centered on strong social and academic contracts that compelled compliance. As the researchers explained:

> Focus schools concentrate on *student outcomes* before all other matters. Zoned schools focus primarily on delivering programs and following procedures.

> Focus schools have *strong social contracts* that communicate the reciprocal responsibilities of administration, students, and teachers and establish the benefits that each derives from fulfilling the contract faithfully. Zoned schools try whenever possible to let staff and students define their own roles in the school.

Table 4.1. Student Responses by Type of School.

	Mean Scores		
	Zoned Public	Focused Public	Focused Catholic
I feel safe in the halls of this school.	2.2	3.2	3.2
The school building is kept clean and in good repair.	1.7	3.1	2.9
This school is a nice place to spend the day.	1.7	2.8	2.5
When people find out that I go to this school, they think I am lucky.	1.6	2.4	2.2
When people who don't go here say things about this school, they say positive things.	1.5	2.3	2.0
When I compare it to other schools that I might go to in New York, I am happy that I am at this school.	2.1	3.0	2.8
Attendance here is good; students come to school and go to class.	1.8	2.6	3.1
Students here act respectfully toward the school.	1.6	2.5	2.5
Students here act respectfully toward the teachers.	1.8	2.6	2.7
Students here are happy enough just to pass; they don't worry about doing well.	3.1	2.4	2.6
Students here think it's a good thing to do well in school; they won't think you're uncool just because you get good grades.	2.4	2.8	2.9
Students here take the rules seriously.	1.8	2.4	2.1

Source: Hill, Foster, and Gendler, 1990, pp. 84.

Focus schools have a *strong commitment to parenting*, and aggressively mold student attitudes and values; they emphasize the secular ethics of honesty, reliability, fairness, and respect for others. Zoned schools see themselves primarily as transmitters of information and imparters of skills.

Focus schools have *centripetal curricula* that draw all students toward learning certain core skills and perspectives. Zoned schools distinguish among students in terms of ability and preference, and offer profoundly different curricula to different groups (pp. vii–viii).

The researchers point out that social contracts are more than missions statements. Social contracts implicitly and explicitly explain how principals, teachers, parents, and students will behave so that the school can achieve its goals, protect its values, and preserve its climate and culture. "It is a bargain that the school offers students and staff members, and that they tacitly accept by joining the school community. . . . Focus schools explain the preexisting contract to students when they enroll. The faculty and staff take pains to inform students about the terms of the bargain and persuade skeptical newcomers of its values. Catholic schools in particular aggressively indoctrinate new students to the norms and expectations. Some create big-brother and big-sister programs with older students serving as models and guides. They do not assume that students will automatically fit in, but they do assume that the school can change students' attitudes and behavior" (Hill, Foster, and Gendler, 1990, pp. 38–39).

Though social contracts focus on both the academic and social sides of student life, their effects are typically most readily noticed on the social side—and in particular on issues of student discipline and student behavior in general. Zoned schools, for example, rely heavily on lists of rules and consequences, do's and don'ts, while focused schools lean more toward norms, values, obligations, and commitments. The researchers discussed the differences as follows:

Zoned schools have rules, but they are highly specific and rely on the authority of the school administration rather than on broad principles derived from joint goals and reciprocal obligations. When such narrowly drawn rules are violated, teachers and administrators face a dilemma: they must either apply the rules strictly in every case, or risk discrediting the rules through lenient application. Few choose the former approach, because it requires harsh action against children whose lives are already too difficult. . . . When discipline is based on explicit agreement about the school's mission, and all parties' reciprocal obligations, teachers and administrators can afford to forgive repentant violators, and withhold punishment because leniency does not weaken the actual base upon which rules are founded. Standards rooted in the school's social contract also perform the vital function of teaching students how to live in an organization and respond to legitimate expectations about reliability, reciprocity, and respect for other rights [p. 41].

Though many public schools qualify as focus schools, Catholic schools seem to find it easier to provide the needed focus for schools to be transformed into moral communities. In their important book, *Catholic Schools and the Common Good,* researchers Anthony Bryk, Valerie Lee, and Peter Holland conclude that the advantage of Catholic schools is that they believe they are and try to function as moral enterprises. They strive to teach students to be moral beings, and this purpose provides a seamless focus for their mission, curriculum, and teaching. Other religious and many nonreligious independent schools function similarly. In reviewing this book, Joseph Shives (1994), a public middle-school principal in Ohio, describes how moral voice works in such communities:

From my perspective as a public school principal, Catholic schools and other sectarian schools have an advantage in maintaining discipline with core belief systems that transcend school rules. Although there are rules in Catholic schools, the morality that guides the behavior of students, teachers, and administrators assumes an orderly climate; rules in Catholic schools are part of a larger moral system rooted in the belief of the Catholic religion. Contrast this with the non-religious—even amoral way—in which teachers are expected to teach and principals to administer to public school students. In public schools, student codes of conduct substitute for moral underpinning. Codes of conduct define unacceptable behavior and the punishments that attach to violations, but the codes have no moral purpose larger than the mere maintenance of order. . . . these schools are communally organized with a set of shared values (among students, staff, and parents), a set of shared

activities (curricular and extra-curricular), and a set of social relations among community members. According to the authors, this
communal organization contributes in salubrious, if indirect ways
to student learning [p. 342].

Public schools, too, can become moral enterprises without
becoming religious or otherwise compromising standards implied
by the First Amendment and similar documents that guarantee the
separation of church and state. It is possible, in other words, to be
sacred while remaining secular. Connections, moral voice, and
other Community Theory ideas, for example, appeal not only
because of their ability to compel a higher standard of living and
achievement in schools, but because they come closer to the meaning of democracy intended by our American founders. In Canadian and American societies, conceptions of citizenship can be
viewed thinly or thickly. A thin conception of citizenship emphasizes individual, economic, spiritual, intellectual, and procedural
rights, and encourages each of us to be absorbed in pursuing personal happiness in forms of private life at work, church, family, or
school. A thick view of citizenship, by contrast, honors individual
rights by emphasizing participation in forms of democratic self-gov-
ernment and public service. The preservation of individual rights
and liberties is viewed as being embedded in the ability of citizens
to forge shared commitments to shared ideas that help them live
their lives together in service to the common good. Such rights,
however, cannot be emphasized at the expense of the political liberties guaranteed in such documents as the Canadian Charter of
Rights and Freedoms and the U.S. Bill of Rights. Indeed for individual rights to be guaranteed, the citizenship must make a collective commitment to embody them in action.
    Citizenship in communities values the private pursuit of hap-
piness, but not at the expense of community (Smith, 1993). Applying Community Theory to schools, and particularly encouraging
the development of moral voice, brings balance to this equation
by ensuring individual rights within the context of the common
good. For it is only when rights are viewed as obligations to be embodied by everyone that they become guaranteed for everyone.

Chapter Five

The Roots of
School Leadership

It is hard to talk about the voice of community, and the importance of moral compacts in energizing that voice, without also talking about leadership. And it is hard to talk about school leadership without also talking about the visions of principals. In organizations, the conventional wisdom is that leaders should have visions and then work to shape the organizations they manage in accordance with their visions. Management expert Burt Nanus (1992) states the case this way: "There is no mystery about this. Effective leaders have agendas; they are totally results oriented. They adopt challenging new visions of what is both possible and desirable, communicate their visions, and persuade others to become so committed to these new directions that they are eager to lend their resources and energies to make them happen" (p. 4). Leaders, in other words, work to make *their* visions realities, and this depends on how well they can sell *their* visions to others.

IBM's CEO Lewis Gerstner and his colleagues Roger Semerad, Denis Doyle, and William Johnston (1994) share this *gesellschaft* view of vision. They rely on Harvard Business School Professor John Kotten's views by recommending that leaders must be able to "devise and articulate a vision; set a strategy for achieving it; build a network of people who agree with and can accomplish the vision; and motivate these people (and others outside the organization) to work hard to realize the vision" (p. 119). They point out that "organizations that are consistency successful, on the battlefield or in the marketplace, pay careful attention to finding and nurturing people [leaders] who can do these things" (p. 119).

Nanus, Gerstner, and Kotten may have the right conception of leadership for corporations and other *gesellschaft* organizations. Their view of leadership seems to make sense when the sources of authority for what is done are embodied in formal organization policies and ideologies, and are embodied in the purposes and personalities of leaders. In *Moral Leadership,* I referred to these two sources of authority as bureaucratic and personal (Sergiovanni, 1992, p. 30).

Leadership practices based on bureaucratic and personal authority are variations of a strategy that emphasizes *follow me.* In the first case it is "Follow me because of my position in the school and the system of bureaucratic roles, rules, and expectations that I represent." In the second case it is "Follow me because I will make it worth your while if you do by trading need-fulfillment and other rewards for compliance." Community Theory forces us to understand leadership differently. The emphasis in community leadership is building a shared followership and the emphasis in building a shared followership is not on *who* to follow, but on *what* to follow. Community members are not asked to comply in response to clever leadership processes or in response to aspects of the leader's personality. They are asked to respond to substance. Leadership in communities is idea based. And the goal of idea-based leadership is to develop a broad-based commitment to shared values and conceptions that become a compelling source of authority for what people must do.

In establishing idea-based leadership, principals have a special responsibility to share their visions of what schools can become, but they must do this in an invitational mode, not in the command or sell modes usually advocated by business writers. Why is an invitational mode right for schools, and why are the command and sell modes wrong for schools? Because school leadership should be directed to connecting parents, teachers, and students morally to each other, and to their responsibilities as defined by shared purposes. In schools, moral connections cannot be commanded by hierarchy or sold by personalities, but must be compelled by helping people to accept their responsibilities.

The moral aspects of school leadership are important because schools function as extensions of families, and principals and teachers function *in loco parentis.* Principals and teachers are stewards who accept responsibility for students and school on behalf of parents. In doing so, they promise to keep the interests of students at heart. Schools have other moral purposes as well. They have, for example, a public obligation to cultivate civic responsibility. They function to ensure the maintenance of certain democratic principles and traditions key to the long-term survival of our society. This civic responsibility must not only be taught to children, but must be modeled in how schools are organized and run. Our commitment to democratic values provides still another reason why vision must be understood differently in schools, and why leadership must be practiced differently in schools.

What schools should not do is function as businesses. And school leaders should not function as owners of businesses. It may have been perfectly acceptable, for example, for Ray Kroc—owner of the McDonald's chain—to have had a vision of how restaurants should function, or to have had a vision of what hamburgers should taste like, and then to work to make that vision a reality. But because of the moral place of schools in our society, principals must be as concerned with the visions of parents, teachers, and students; with the visions implicit in our democratic traditions; and indeed with the visions embodied in Judeo-Christian values as they are with their own visions. Moral covenants for schools in our democratic society are forged as many visions are shared and brought together.

Most of us are not accustomed to thinking in terms of vision. Certainly parents, teachers, and students have visions, but they are implicitly held. It is up to principals to get the vision conversation started, and to keep it going. A place to begin is for them to talk about their values and the hopes and dreams that they have for the school. Roland Barth (1990) suggests that principals can ask teachers to recall the visions they once had, but are now dimmed by the realities of teaching in *gesellschaft* schools. They can help teachers struggle to restore these visions, and they then can commit themselves to enabling this restoration. Principals might ask, For our visions to be realized, what changes would have to take place in the way we organize and operate our school? In the way we understand leadership? How should we live our lives together in our school? How should our responsibilities be shared, and what commitments must we make? Parents, too, need to be encouraged to talk about the kinds of schools they want for their children, and parents need to be invited to join in the struggle to make these schools real.

Tensions are likely to emerge as different people come together to share their visions, and to attempt to reach a harmonious agreement. While parents want community for their children, they often have a hard time thinking about things in ways other than the more selfish sense of "what is best for my own child." Teachers want to do the best they can for the school, but are faced with managing the realities of conflicting demands, overcommitments, and shortages of time and resources that are endemic in today's schools. And principals are under enormous pressure to hurry things along—to make visible progress within short, and often unrealistic, time frames. For these reasons the sharing of visions is helpful, but not enough. This sharing must take place within the broader web of roles and responsibilities that connects everyone to still another moral perspective—the perspective of obligations and duties that come from accepting certain roles.

Madeline Cartwright, the now-famous principal of Philadelphia's Blaine School during the eighties, believed that when roles are understood as responsibilities, they speak to us in a moral voice (Cartwright, 1993). As principal, she was quick to point out that teachers cannot meet their responsibilities to students if parents do not meet their parental responsibilities. And she noted that it is hard for parents to meet their responsibilities if teachers fail to meet their responsibilities as teachers. Students, too, are part of this moral web of responsibilities. Try as hard as teachers or parents might, neither are likely to be successful if students do not hold up their end. "Success for any of us is success for all of us" was how Cartwright viewed things (p. 106).

In *After Virtue* (1981), the philosopher Alasdair MacIntyre points out that the connection of roles to obligations is a key feature of community life. This feature is less evident in today's *gesellschaft* world, but it was once well established in traditional society. What a person did was readily judged by all community members in terms of the standards appropriate to her or his role.

Applying this traditional view of roles and obligations to schools means that a parent who leaves a preschool child at home alone, or who does not get school-aged children to bed at a decent hour, fails morally in meeting her or his role responsibilities as a parent. Similarly, teachers who do not prepare lessons adequately or who do not strive to learn more about their craft, and students who cheat or evade their assigned work also fail morally in meeting role responsibilities. As Walter Feinberg (1993) explains, "In taking a role, they have made a promise to fulfill the virtues appropriate to it. In rejecting the virtues, they have broken the promise" (p. 43).

Feinberg notes that in today's *gesellschaft* society, individuals are separated from their roles by being allowed to determine what is moral or not as a question of individual conscience rather than accepting what is considered to be moral as a consensual understanding of the community. Both individual conscience and consensual understandings are important. In Community Theory, however, the balance between the two is struck somewhere on the side of consensual understanding, but not so far on this side that individual conscience has no role to play. In communities, rights and responsibilities do not stand alone, but become parts of a common web of meaning.

In practice, the equating of roles with responsibilities means that teachers, parents, principals, and students have certain responsibilities and duties that they are obliged to embody because these are the right things to do. Good teachers, for example, are concerned about the individual needs of their students. Good teachers do not give up on their students. Good teachers are prepared, and work as hard as they can to teach as well as they can. Good parents and other caretakers ensure that students have an opportunity and place to do their homework. Good parents and other caretakers set limits as to how long children should stay up. And, allowing for maturation levels, good students must hold up their end of the moral bargain as well. Schools as moral communities have an obligation to teach students these lessons of role responsibility.[1]

---

[1] Though no easy answers exist to the parental role responsibilities problems that often arise from large numbers of teenage parents, and from large numbers of other families under pressure, schools must do what they can to teach and to enable parental responsibility. Together with other agencies, and under the umbrella of the right national policies, we can expect even single thirteen-year-old fathers and mothers to accept personal responsibility for their parental roles.

The Roots of School Leadership

Community Theory takes us to the roots of school leadership. Leadership is generally viewed as a process of getting a group to take action that embodies the leader's purposes (as is typically the case in business organizations) or shared purposes (as should be the case in schools). Leadership is different from commanding or bribing compliance in that it involves influencing others by persuasion or example, or by tapping inner moral forces. This influence, however, is typically reciprocal. Unless followers are willing to be led, leaders can't lead. Further, groups naturally create norms that constitute a cultural order or way of life. Leaders must be part of that order even as they attempt to change it, or their leadership will be rejected. Faced with either the fear or reality of rejection they resort to commanding or requiring compliance. But when they do this, follower commitment is sacrificed, and compliance is difficult to maintain over time.

For leadership to work, leaders and followers need to be tied together by a consensual understanding that mediates this pattern of reciprocal influence. The well-respected commentator on leadership, John Gardner (1986a), explains:

> It is in this context that leaders arise; and it is this context that determines what kinds of leaders will emerge and what will be expected of them. A loyal constituency [followership] is won when people, consciously or unconsciously, judge the leader to be capable of solving their problems and meeting their needs, when the leader is seen as symbolizing their norms, and when their image of the leader (whether or not it corresponds to reality) is congruent with their inner environment of myth and legend [p. 11].

In schools, this reciprocal process of leaders and followers influencing each other to action involves not only issues of shared purposes, but involves, as discussed earlier, roles that are connected to moral obligations. Just as teachers, parents, and students have roles linked to moral obligations, principals are expected to meet the obligations that come from their role responsibilities as leaders.

It is through morally held role responsibilities that we can understand school administration as a profession in the more traditional sense. School administration is bound not just to standards of technical competence, but, to use the distinction drawn by Bellah and his colleagues (1985, p. 290), to *standards of public obligation* as well. Standards of public obligation always override technical standards when the two are in conflict. Were these standards from traditional leadership fully applied to business organizations, then the self-interests of corporations would always be second to public obligations—an unlikely development that would undermine market principles, and that would revolutionize business administration.

At the root of the principal's role responsibilities we find the roots of school leadership—a commitment to administer to the needs of the school as an institution by serving its purposes, by serving those who struggle to embody these purposes, and by acting as a guardian to protect the institutional integrity of the school. The first roles of principals, as we shall soon discuss, are ministerial ones.

How do principals embody their ministerial roles in practice? What are the tasks that principals should perform as leaders? The following nine tasks are worth considering:[2]

Purposing—bringing together shared visions into a covenant that speaks compellingly to principals, teachers, parents, and students with a moral voice.

Maintaining harmony—building a consensual understanding of school purposes, of how the school should function, and of the moral connections between roles and responsibilities while respecting individual conscience and individual style differences.

Institutionalizing values—translating the school's covenant into a workable set of procedures and structures that facilitates the accomplishment of school purposes, and that provides norm systems for directing and guiding behavior.

Motivating—providing for the basic psychological needs of members on the one hand, and for the basic cultural needs of mem-

---

[2] See John W. Gardner (1986b) for a similar though more general list. He includes envisioning goals, affirming values, managing, achieving a workable level of unity, explaining, serving as a symbol, representing the group externally, and renewing.

bers to experience sensible and meaningful school lives on the other.

Managing—ensuring the necessary day-to-day support (planning, organizing, agenda setting, mobilizing resources, providing procedures, record keeping, and so on) that keeps the school running effectively and efficiently.

Explaining—giving reasons for asking members to do certain things, and giving explanations that link what members are doing to the larger picture.

Enabling—removing obstacles that prevent members from meeting their commitments on the one hand, and providing resources and support to help members to meet their commitments on the other.

Modeling—accepting responsibility as head follower of the school's covenant by modeling purposes and values in thought, word, and action.

Supervising—providing the necessary oversight to ensure the school is meeting its commitments, and when it is not, to find out why, and to help everyone do something about it.

Most of these tasks are understandable, but the "supervising" task may need some explaining. The word *supervision,* for example, has a *gesellschaft* tinge that conjures up factory images of "snoopervising" foremen checking up on workers. But supervision was originally a virtuous word that referred to the carrying out of one's stewardship responsibilities. Traditionally, stewardship meant the overseeing and caring for an institution such as a university, church, or school.

When principals function as stewards by providing for the oversight and care of their schools, they are not so much managers or executives as they are administrators. According to Webster, to *manage* means to handle, to control, to make submissive, to direct affairs, to achieve one's purposes. Webster defines an *executive* as an individual or group designated to control or direct an organization. *Administer,* by contrast, means to serve, to minister, and to "superintend the execution, use, or conduct of" an enterprise. *Superintend,* in turn, means to attend to, give attention to, have oversight over what is intended. It means, in other words, supervision. As supervisor, the principal acts *in loco parentis* in relationship to students, ensuring that all is well for them. As supervisor, the principal acts as a trustee in relationship to parents ensuring that all is well for them too. And as supervisor, the principal acts as steward, guarding and protecting the school's purposes and structures.

Much of the literature on school supervision tries to provide for the care and oversight of teaching and learning in schools, but is hampered by being too connected to the kind of supervision found in *gesellschaft* organizations. Needed is a new definition of supervision that reclaims its original intent. Instead of looking to business organizations, we might begin this process of reclamation by trying to understand how supervision is defined and how it functions in churches, families, youth associations, mutual help societies, and other *gemeinschaft* enterprises that have been less influenced by business values. We might, for example, look to pastoral supervision to see what insights might be useful in helping us to develop a supervision unique to the school.

Kenneth Pohly, director of the Center for Supervisory Studies of the United Theological Seminary, defines pastoral supervision as "doing and reflecting on ministry in which a supervisor (teacher) and one or more supervisees (learners) covenant together to reflect critically on their ministry as a way of growing in self-awareness, ministering competence, theological understanding, and christian commitment" (1993, p. 75). In schools, we might read "theological understanding, and christian commitment" to mean an idea structure based on teaching and learning and other school issues that translates readily into the traditions and shared values that comprise the school's covenant as it becomes a community.

Pohly believes that supervision is pastoral, is a way of doing ministry, is covenantal, is reflective, and is intentional. It is pastoral "in the sense of its shepherding nature, that is, its care-giving. This includes everyone involved—supervisees as well as supervisors. The giving and receiving of care is something in which all supervisory participants engage." It is a way of doing ministry because "it provides a way for persons to engage in the same ministry as colleagues, as co-participants." It is covenantal in the sense that it "occurs within an agreement in which persons say to each other: 'This is what we will do together, and for which we will hold one another accountable.'" It is reflective because "it occurs within a supervisory conversation in which the participants reflect critically upon their ministry." And it is intentional as it seeks to help people understand themselves more clearly, to assist them in developing their competencies, clarifying their understandings, and in deepening their commitments to the enterprise (Pohly, 1993, pp. 75–76).

Supervision in communities implies accountability, but not in the tough, inspectoral sense suggested by factory images of inspection and control. Instead, it implies an accountability embedded in tough and tender caring. Principals care enough about the school, about the values and purposes that undergird it, about the students they serve, about the parents they represent, about the teachers upon whom they depend, that they will do whatever is necessary to *protect* school values and purposes on the one hand, and to *enable* their accomplishment on the other.

In a recent interview, Deborah Meier, co-director of the celebrated Central Park East Secondary School in New York City, was asked, "What is the role of the principal in an effective school?" Her response shows how the various ministerial roles of the principal are brought together by supervision understood as an expression of stewardship (Scherer, 1994):

> Someone has to keep an eye on the whole and alert everyone when parts need close- or long-range attention. A principal's job is to put forth to the staff an agenda. The staff may or may not agree, but they have an opportunity to discuss it. I'll say, "Listen, I've been around class after class, and I notice this, don't notice this, we made a commitment to be accountable for one another, but I didn't see anybody visiting anybody else's class. . . ." Paul [Schwartz, Meier's co-director] and I also read all the teacher's assessments of students. Once we noticed that the 9th and the 10th math teachers often said the kids didn't seem to have an aptitude for math. We asked the math staff, "How can these kids do nicely in 7th and 8th grade, and then seem inept in 9th and 10th? Are we fooling ourselves in 7th and 8th, or are we fooling ourselves in 9th and 10th? Because they are the same kids" [p. 7].

Meier and Schwartz both practice leadership that is idea based. The sources of authority they appeal to are the values that are central to the school, and the commitments that everyone has made to them. And because of this, their supervisory responsibilities do not compromise democratic principles, dampen teacher empowerment, or get in the way of community building. Both directors are committed to creating a staff-run school with high standards—one where staff must know each other, be familiar with each other's work, and know how the school operates. As Meier (1992) explains, "Decisions are made as close to each teacher's own classroom setting as possible, although all decisions are ultimately the responsibility of the whole staff. The decisions are not merely on minor matters—length of classes or the number of field trips. The teachers collectively decide on content, pedagogy, and assessment as well. They teach what they think matters . . . governance is simple. There are virtually no permanent standing committees. Finally, we work together to develop assessment systems for our students, their families, ourselves, and the broader public. Systems that represent our values and beliefs in as direct a manner as possible" (p. 607).

Of course a principal can't be tough about values, standards, role responsibilities, and meeting commitments without also being tender by accepting responsibility for enabling teachers to meet their commitments. Central Park East Secondary School works hard to do just that by providing for structures and other arrangements that enable teachers to reflect on their own teaching, and the teaching of their colleagues, and to give each other support (Meier, 1991, p. 144).

Leadership as Pedagogy

With supervision as an expression of stewardship at the core, the tasks of leadership are brought together when principals and other school leaders practice leadership as a form of pedagogy. *Pedagogy* is not a term in popular use in North America, and when it is used it refers vaguely to instruction, curriculum, or teaching. But the term has deep historical roots and meanings that are worth reviving. As Max van Manen explains, "The term *pedagogue* derives from the Greek, and refers not to the teacher, but to the watchful slave or guardian whose responsibility it was to lead *(agogos)* the young boy *(paides)* to school. . . . The adult had the task of accompanying the child, of being with the child, of caring for the child. The pedagogue would be expected to see to it that the child stayed out of trouble, and behaved properly. This is a kind of 'leading' that often walks *behind* the one who is led. The slave or pedagogue was there *in loco parentis*" (p. 37).

The pedagogue's job, be she or he a teacher, principal, coach, guardian, slave, or other adult, was to provide the child with a sense of protection, direction, and orientation—a role shared with parents, and a role exercised in their absence. And since this role was so important to the development of the best interest of the child, and to the protection of the interests of parents, it implied a form of leadership. "The original Greek idea of pedagogy had associated with it the meaning of *leading* in the sense of accompanying the child and living with the child in such a way as to provide direction and care for his or her life" (van Manen, 1991, p. 38). Teachers practice a form of pedagogical leadership directly since in schools they stand first and closest in a caring relationship to children. They have the major responsibility for guiding children academically, socially, and spiritually through the world of childhood to adulthood. Indeed, the process of education in itself implies leadership. Children, as van Mannen explains, must eventually grow out of (*educere:* to lead out of) the world of childhood, and adults must help children grow into (*educare:* to lead into) the world of adulthood (p. 38).

Principals practice leadership as a form of pedagogy by facilitating this process, and by ensuring that the interests of children are served well. A key part of this practice is the ability of the leader to mobilize people and community to face their problems, and to make progress in solving them (Heifetz, 1994). In this sense, the pedagogy they practice is understood as a form of authority that ensures that people make good decisions and face up to their responsibilities, and that things work right for children. This pedagogical authority is not authoritarian in the sense that it is exercised simply because principals have more power than teachers or students, but it is authoritative. Its legitimacy comes in part from the virtuous responsibilities associated with the principal's role, and in part from the principal's obligation to function as the head follower of the school's moral compact.

Principals also practice leadership as a form of pedagogy when they engage in the important task of purposing. Philip Selznik (1957) explains:

The inbuilding of purpose . . . involves transforming men and groups from neutral, technical units into participants who have a peculiar stamp, sensitivity, and commitment. This is ultimately an educational process. It has been well said that the effective leader must know the meaning and master the techniques of the educator. As in the larger community, education is more than narrow technical training; though it does not shrink from indoctrination, it also teaches men to think for themselves. The leader as educator requires an ability to interpret the role and character of the enterprise, to perceive and develop models for thought and behavior, and to find modes of communication that will inculcate general rather than merely partial perspectives [pp. 149–150].

This pedagogical process leads to the "institutional embodiment of purpose" that must occur if schools as communities are to speak to teachers, parents, and students in a moral voice.

It is not enough for leaders just to make the right moves for any purpose that suits them, or for any vision that they might have of what schools should be like. The noted historian and leadership theorist, James Mac Gregor Burns (1978), pointed out that purposes and visions should be socially useful, should serve the common good, should meet the needs of followers, and should elevate followers to a higher moral level. He calls this kind of leadership *transformational*. Many business writers and their imitators in educational administration have secularized Burns's original definition of Transformational Leadership to make it more suitable to the values of *gesellschaft* organizations. They "conceive of transformation" not in Burns's sense of elevating the moral functioning of a polity, but in the sense of inspiration, intellectual stimulation, and personal considerations . . . or altering the basic normative principals that guide an institution . . ." (Heifetz, 1994, pp. 288–289; see also Bass, 1985, and Hargrove, 1989). This revisionist concept of Transformational Leadership might be alright for managers and CEOs in business organizations, but when it comes to practicing leadership in their children's schools, few business persons are likely to prefer it over Burns's original definition.

Ronald Heifetz (1994) believes that leadership is inescapably normative. He explains:

We have to take sides. When we teach, write about, and model the exercise of leadership, we inevitably support or challenge people's conceptions of themselves, their roles, and most importantly their ideas about how social systems make progress on problems. Leadership is a normative concept because implicit in people's notions of leadership are images of a social contract. Imagine the differences in behavior when people operate with the idea that "leadership means influencing the community to follow the leader's vision" versus "leadership means influencing the community to face its problems". In the first instance, influence is the mark of leadership; a leader gets people to accept his vision, and communities address people's problems by looking to him. If something goes wrong, the fault lies with the leader. In the second, progress on problems is the measure of leadership; leaders mobilize people to face problems, and communities make progress on problems because leaders challenge and help them do so. If something goes wrong, the fault lies with both leaders and the community [pp. 14–15].

Heifetz, who directs the Leadership Education Project at Harvard's Kennedy School of Government, believes that mobilizing people to tackle tough problems is at the heart of leadership. To him, mobilization connotes motivating, organizing, orienting and focusing attention on problems, and problem solving. Mobilizing the school community on behalf of problem solving is practicing leadership as a form of pedagogy.

When principals practice leadership as pedagogy, they exercise their stewardship responsibilities by committing themselves to building, to serving, to caring for, and to protecting the school and its purposes. Practicing leadership as pedagogy asks a great deal of leaders and followers alike. It calls both to higher levels of commitment. It calls both to higher levels of goodness. It calls both to higher levels of effort. And it calls both to higher levels of accountability.

Do we have the capacity to respond to the calling of pedagogy? I think so. Will we be able to respond perfectly? I doubt it. We are, after all, an imperfect lot, with our own needs, our own fears, and our own concerns. These imperfections will always get in the way. No matter how imperfect we are, however, we will be better off (as will the schools we serve) if we are eager to try, if we are willing to take up the struggle, and if we view our efforts as a lifelong quest to improve the common good. Robert W. Terry (1993), a thoughtful commentator on leadership, provides some words that can help us when the going gets rough:

> Leadership lives at the intersection of the authentic and the inauthentic, tilting the world toward the authentic. Leadership is always mindful of that, as we call forth authenticity, we can never forget that the conflicts and ambiguities of action reside not just in the world but also within ourselves. No one arrives with pure motives or unambiguous interests. The struggles for authenticity are within and without—the ultimate congruence of our actions is unknown. Good intentions can lead to unintended suffering. Bad intentions, at times, can produce unexpected good results. Faith in authenticity must undergird our actions. To be faithful, we must believe that any authentic act, no matter how small or seemingly insignificant, is upheld by the universe as worthy and honorable. Leadership is spiritually grounded. To lose this hope and this faith is to despair and to fall into cynicism. Leadership is indeed a noble calling worthy of our most profound commitment. For what we do, in the final analysis, rests solely on our faith that our actions in our families, communities, associations, institutions, and the world contribute to the well being of all those we touch and serve [p. 274].

The roots of school leadership reach not only into the moral voice of community and the ministerial role of the principal, but reach as well to our own personal commitments as parents, teachers, and principals to do the right thing for our children; to accept as part of our role responsibilities the necessity to practice leadership as a form of pedagogy. Aristotle would suggest that nothing could be more natural for schools since he defined pedagogy as a *good*; as a *virtue*. To MacIntyre (1981), a virtue is an acquired human quality that enables us to provide those conditions and to achieve those purposes that serve the common good. In teaching and other practices, virtue requires a commitment to standards of excellence that define teaching, as well as a commitment to justice, to courage, and to honesty (p. 178). This quest for virtue involves selflessly building and serving a community. "Moreover, specific virtues facilitate, but are also intrinsic to, this enterprise: honesty, fairness, reliability, consistency, obedience to law, courage, courtesy, judgement, among others. These virtues make it possible to work together; to create friendships not solely on the shifting sands of affection, but on the sure foundation of partnership and shared accomplishment. An individual human being, especially an individual obsessed with his or her own pleasure and well-being, is a functional and miserable individual. But a human being . . . a member of a family and a larger political community, can achieve 'merit,' 'honor,' 'harmony,' and 'purposefulness'" (Lewis, 1990). It is this quest for community toward which the roots of school leadership must be directed. It is not enough to want to do the right thing. We must have the will to take up the challenge of school leadership as our life calling. The essence of leadership is, after all, action. "Faith, without works, is dead" (James 2:17).

| The Case for Smaller Schools

Newspapers across the country recently carried the following story:

> The lockers are being bolted shut, and backpacks are being banned next month at Wilson Junior High School in an attempt to ease crowding and campus crime.

> Instead of having to haul around textbooks, students will be given a set to keep at home, and classrooms will contain another set for use at the . . . school. . . . [The principal] hopes the plan will lessen congestion during class changes; cut tardiness; reduce hiding places for guns, drugs, and other contraband; eliminate locker thefts; decrease the number of lost books; and help forgetful students. . . . Though bolting the lockers won't provide more space . . . [the principal] believes it will ease the hallway crowding since students won't be huddled in hallways around lockers between classes.

> "It's not a panacea, but it's a step in the right direction," he said. . . . The . . . School Board's decision to plunk down an additional twenty-five thousand in local tax money to pay for duplicate books also comes at a time when the state has announced it is short 100 million dollars to pay for updated textbooks [Associated Press, 1994, p. 9–A].

In the San Antonio area, several school districts have adopted Zero Tolerance Discipline Management programs that require automatic expulsion of students for certain offenses. Some districts are equipping schools with hidden video cameras to curb misbehavior. "Ten video cameras and sixty metal-box mounts have been installed in sixty buses. The cameras will be moved from bus to bus regularly so students won't know when they are actually being video-taped. . . . The video-tapes will be reviewed regularly, and can be used as evidence in student disciplinary actions" (Martinez, 1994, p. 5–B). One San Antonio area school district now requires junior and senior high school students to carry only transparent backpacks and transparent book bags so that contents are visible.

Imagine the shock and indignation we and our parents would feel if these were the banner newspaper stories when we went to school. Two sets of books? Locked lockers? Transparent book bags? Yet in this age of school district police forces and school metal detectors, news stories such as these hardly garner a second thought. What else are school administrators to do?

Today's world is different from yesterday's world. The level of violence is up. Kids seem more alienated. Gangs are more dangerous. Drug and alcohol abuse is on the increase. Student subcultures are more insular and distant, and everyone seems to care less. The bottom line for most school administrators is that today's kids are more difficult to control. Harsher times call for more desperate measures. Thus banning lockers and backpacks, furnishing students with two sets of books, adopting Zero Tolerance Discipline policies, and using video cameras on buses may make sense, given the problem that schools face. As long as we have these problems, we will have to spend more and more of our scarce time and resources on these desperate measures to control students.

The catch-22 in all of this is that with resources limited, every dollar and every minute schools spend on student control is a dollar and minute schools are not able to spend on teaching and learning. Every assistant principal, dean of discipline, security officer, hall monitor, guidance counselor, and social worker that we must hire to work on control issues is a person we do not have to work on teaching and learning issues. Perhaps we must do what we are now doing to get through today. But for tomorrow, we need thoughtful and practical strategies that will not be wasteful of our financial and human resources, and that will make schools more effective places for learning.

No easy answers exist, and no easy recipe is available that will make all students eager learners and caring members of their school communities. But one thing seems clear. As long as we continue to use *gesellschaft* theories that promote big schools, that emphasize chains of command, that encourage specialization, departmentalization, and fragmentation, and that require us to spend large amounts of time on crowd control to organize and run our schools, we will be stuck with locked lockers, video cameras, and transparent backpacks. Whatever else we do to improve schools, building community must be part of our strategy. And building community leads us to reconsider the issue of school size.

Chapter Three defined *community* as collections of people bonded together by mutual commitments and special relationships, who together are bound to a set of shared ideas and values that they believe in, and feel compelled to follow. This bonding and binding helps them to become members of a tightly knit web of meaningful relationships with moral overtones. In communities of this kind, people belong, people care, people help each other, people make and keep commitments, people feel responsible for themselves, and responsible to others.

Two conditions help to develop the bonding and binding necessary for community building—continuity of place, and manageable scale. It is easier for small schools to provide both. Thus the size of a school can become a key leverage point for helping to make transparent backpacks and surveillance video cameras unnecessary. The size of the school can become a key leverage point for helping students become eager learners and committed members of their school communities. *Small size in itself is not enough.* Small size is, nonetheless, a necessary condition for bringing about the changes we want.

Using "Catcher" in J. D. Salinger's novel *Catcher in the Rye* as her metaphor for rescuing children in need, school superintendent Joanne Yatvin (1994) states the case this way:

> Because we are where children are, because they will drive us crazy if we do nothing, and because we care, educators must be today's catchers in the rye.
>
> I have lost faith in any and all large-scale, organized solutions to educational problems. They just put more paperwork, regulations, and job titles between children and the help they need. Where schools are failing, it is not because they don't have enough projects and programs, but because they have lost the human touch. Children mired in the morass of family and community decay can't benefit from red ribbons, higher standards, or instructional technology; they need caring adults to pull them out of the muck and set them

on solid ground one at a time. . . . The framework of operation must be small, physically close to children, and flexible. Forget any plan for recruiting five hundred teachers as catchers, training them, and setting up a schedule for patrolling the rye. We need small schools or schools that are divided into small community units; classroom time, space, and organization that allows personal relationships to flourish; legitimacy for play and conversation in schools; authority in the hands of front-line practitioners; and educational visions unclouded by political pressure to cover academic ground, raise test scores, or produce workers for industry [p. 37].

[Once the scale is down and relationships are more personal,] educators are able to catch children who stray too close to the edge. They know each child as an individual, and see most of the things that are happening to them. Children hang around and tell them what they cannot see. Educators find time to talk to each other and time to teach children about the world without having to "implement" or "assess" anything. They can make exceptions to rules and change foolish ones. They can do things differently. When the behavior of children or of bureaucrats becomes intolerable, teachers can even stamp their feet and yell, "this has got to stop" [p. 37].

Small schools can take many forms. Some schools can be housed in their own small free-standing buildings designed or remodeled to handle fewer students. But today's large school buildings will not disappear just because smaller schools make sense. To deal with this problem, the traditional definition of school defined by brick and mortar—a definition that equates a single school with a single school building—will have to be abandoned. Instead, schools should be defined as small collections of people who are committed to each other, and who are connected to similar values and ideas. In this definition, common connections from shared commitments and values, not common bricks, are the ingredients that make a school. Thus in any school building there might be several quite independent schools functioning side by side as learning communities—each unique in its purposes, but each the same in the loyalty and commitment it asks of its members.

At first glance, having several free-standing schools sharing the same building raises important questions. How will all of these different and independent schools be managed? How will resources be shared? What do we do about the football team, the band, and other sports and activities? Who will be responsible for the cafeteria? To which school will the librarian be assigned? Who reports to whom? How will we decide which students and teachers go where?

I don't have the answers to these questions. The various schools that share the same building will have to work things out. Most central offices are filled with well-trained and bright people who can help. The issue is not one of talent, but commitment. If we want to, we can find the solutions we need to make size an advantage rather than a disadvantage.

One model worth thinking about is that of an office building. Imagine one where a detective agency shares the first floor with a dentist's office. The second floor is occupied by an insurance company. A real estate agency is on the third floor. Three more dentists are on the fourth floor. The lower level is now vacant, but available for rent. Each of the enterprises that occupy this office building operates quite independently. Though all are required to follow the same health and safety codes and civil rights laws, they have their own purposes, they set their own calendar and hours, and they hire, evaluate and develop their own employees. Further, they have their own dress codes, ways of doing things, and other nuances of culture. Yet they share the same parking lot, maintenance staff, elevator service, security, and cafeteria. I don't think we would have any problems working things out if we rented that lower-level space for an alternative school, or for an elementary school that serves downtown commuters. So why would it be different if we rented or owned the whole building, and put a different school on each floor? As to answering the question of which students and which teachers will go where, why not let them decide for themselves? That seems to work for the four dentists and their patients that occupy separate parts of the office building.

But Are Small Schools More Effective?

From a community perspective, it is easy to argue for small schools. Nearly everyone agrees that both our schools and our society have a connections problem. And nearly everyone agrees that one way to renew connections is to help schools to become caring communities. Further, few dispute the claim that getting the scale down helps accomplish this goal. For example, as Stanford Professor Nel Noddings (1992) points out, "In order to build a caring community students need continuity in their school residence. They should stay in one school building for longer than two or three years. Children need time to settle in, to become responsible for their physical surroundings, to take part in maintaining a caring community. When we have to choose between highly specialized programs for a narrow range and a continuity of place, we should choose the latter" (p. 66). Continuity of place is easier to achieve in smaller schools, and in larger schools that deliberately think small and act small.

The link between caring and learning is a tight one. Students, for example, do things for people they like and trust. In caring communities, this pattern of liking and trusting is much more apt to be constructive and beneficial to students than is the case in more *gesellschaft* schools. Large, impersonal schools force students to look to themselves to get their needs met. The norms of the student subculture and the youth culture at large begin to strengthen beyond reason, and soon take over. The consequences are not always good. Though relationships are complex, they ultimately affect learning. Noddings explains:

> Students will do things for people they like and trust. This is a fact that we must acknowledge. There is a worrisome side to it. Kids will do dreadful things as well as beautiful ones for leaders they trust; they will do trivial and menial things as well as significant ones. And to make that more complex, they will not *always* meekly follow those they trust; sometimes they rebel. Further, they often transfer love and trust thoughtlessly. Thus there are untrustworthy forms of "love" and even of "trust".

> Despite all of this complexity, there is a vital nucleus of educational meaning here. Kids learn in communion. They listen to people who matter to them, and to whom they matter. The patterns of ignorance we deplore are signs that kids and adults are not talking to each other about everyday life, and the cultural forms once widely shared. How can it be that kids who watch television every night do not know where El Salvador or the Philippines or Israel is? The people telling the news do not matter, and if there is not a caring parent to comment on the news, then none of it matters.

> So, at bottom, subject matter cannot carry itself. Relation, except in very rare cases, precedes any engagement with subject matter. Caring relations can prepare students for an initial receptivity to all sorts of experience and subject matters [Noddings, 1992, p. 36].

In his monumental work *A Place Called School,* John Goodlad (1984) concluded that the burden of proof is on *large* size. His data revealed that "Most of the schools clustering in the top group of our sample were small, compared with the schools clustering near the bottom. It is not impossible to have a good large school; it is simply more difficult" (p. 309). The smallest schools in his sample were better at solving their problems, were more intellectually oriented, had more caring teachers, and had higher levels of parent and student satisfaction.

After reviewing the research on the effectiveness of small schools, Tom Gregory (1992) concludes "the literature demonstrates that students learn at least as much in small high schools as they do in large ones, that they are less likely to drop out of them, and that schools cost little more to operate" (p. 4). He cites Fowler's research on New Jersey high schools as an example. Fowler concluded that "public school size and district size both influence schooling outcomes [in favor of small size], and although other evidence of this relationship has accumulated, policy makers seem to ignore the findings and its significance" (Fowler, 1989, p. 21; quoted in Gregory, 1992, p. 4).

Gregory points out that the research record in favor of small schools is particularly impressive when one takes into account that "These favorable comparisons were achieved in small high schools which typically function under the handicap of attempting to emulate a big-school model, and these results were achieved in schools which my own experience has led me to believe are still too big to enjoy the essential advantages that are available only to very small high schools" (p. 4).

Though the issue of how small is small enough is yet to be resolved, it does appear that significant reduction in scale, not only of schools, but even in the size of school districts, can help. Walberg and Walberg (1994), for example, examined data from thirty-eight states to see if links existed between size and student achievement of both schools and school districts. Viadero (1994b) summarizes the Walbergs' research as follows:

> States with larger schools and districts—and states that pay a larger share of education spending—tend to have lower student achieve-

ment. This holds true, the researchers say, even after taking into account socio-economic factors and per-pupil spending in those states.

"To some extent educators have imitated business people" says the elder Walberg, a research professor of education at The University of Illinois at Chicago . . . it was thought at one time that bigger business would be better, and it was thought that it would be cheaper.

But for schools, the Walbergs conclude in their report "the centralizing trends of the past half century point in the wrong direction".

Why do rural schools in Iowa and other Western and Midwestern states consistently attain the highest SAT scores in the nation? According to "The Report Card on American Education," a study conducted by the American Legislative Exchange Council (New York Times Service, 1994), the answer is that rural schools are small. "The study found that school size, not classroom size, was the key in the performance of students. Children do better in places small enough that 'the principal knows the name of each student'." Schools with fewer than 300 students showed the best performance . . . even though class size in many of these schools was higher than the national average" (p. 6–M).

In *Big School, Small School,* Roger Barker and Paul Gump (1964) reported that students in smaller schools were more eager to learn, and more likely to participate in school activities. In their view, a school should be small enough so that all of its students not only feel needed, but are needed to make the school work. Small schools are able to call on students in such a way that their school lives have more sense and meaning. Picking up on the theme, Judith Kleinfeld (1993) points out that one important advantage of small schools is that they create "undermanned settings." Such settings are places where there are not enough people to fit all the roles that are available. As a result, more is asked of everyone. Risk-taking is more accepted. More opportunities for leadership become available. And one's learning curve remains forever steep as new challenges must be accepted, and new ideas mastered. Today, everyone is talking about schools becoming learning communities—places where teachers and students together are involved in inquiry and discovery. One way to move beyond talk is to deliberately plan schools that are "undermanned settings" for students and teachers alike.

Kleinfeld writes humorously about life in Alaska as an "undermanned setting," and about the resulting proliferation of characters that parade across the screen in the television program "Northern Exposure." She summarizes, as well, the benefits of such a setting for schools, concluding that students in small schools are not just big fish in small ponds, but actually grow into bigger fish. Her article is worth reading at length:

> *No shortage of characters in the North*
>
> "*Northern Exposure* is fun, but where would you ever find a place with so many characters?" said a friend.
>
> "Come to think of it, I live there!" he said a moment later, thinking of some of the personalities he knew.
>
> Many of us believe Alaska is filled with real characters, people bigger than life, and far more interesting than you'd ever find Outside.
>
> Research on what happens to people who live in "undermanned settings" gives grounds for thinking that the great land may indeed produce great people.
>
> An "undermanned setting" is a place without enough people to fill the available roles.
>
> Certain important and predictable things happen to people in undermanned settings, argue psychologist Roger Barker and his colleagues on the basis of years of research at the University of Kansas.
>
> These include:
>
> 1. Participation in a greater variety of activities. People in sparsely populated settings learn to do things they wouldn't do in larger settings. They become generalists, rather than specialists.
> 2. Involvement in more difficult tasks. People take on challenging tasks they don't know how to do—someone has to do them.
> 3. Greater responsibilities. With fewer people available, more people take on significant roles.
> 4. Less attention paid to differences between individuals. Since everyone is needed or the show won't go on, people become

less critical of each other. People have a lot more freedom to be themselves.

The tasks may not get done as well in an undermanned setting. But the people themselves develop into more competent and interesting personalities.

Paul Gump and Wallace Friesen tested these ideas by examining what happened to students in small rural high schools (with a junior class of 16 to 31) compared to students in a large consolidated high school (with a junior class of 794).

In the small schools, students indeed held more positions of responsibility. They were twice as likely as students in a large school to have a job like working at a concession stand during a football game or playing on the football team.

In the small schools, students were six times as likely to hold central positions, like being president of the student council.

Small high school students also held responsible positions in a wider variety of activities. In a small high school, a basketball player sometimes had to blow the trombone at half time.

When asked what kinds of satisfactions they got from school activities, the small school students reported "more satisfactions related (a) to the development of competence, (b) to being challenged, (c) to engaging in important actions, and (d) to being valued."

They said things like, "I got the speakers for all those meetings" or "It gave me a chance to see how good I am."

The large school students reported more satisfactions resulting from being a spectator and being part of a large group. They said things like, "I enjoyed watching the game", or "I liked mingling with the rest of the crowd."

This study just looked at a few high schools in Kansas. Leonard Band then compared a national sample of 21,000 seniors from high schools of different size.

The smaller the school, the greater the students' achievements in leadership, music, writing, and drama.

People in undermanned settings—whether small schools or sparsely populated places like Alaska—may be more than a big fish in a small pond.

We have reason to believe they actually grow into bigger fishes.

How Small Is Small?

Though nearly all small-school advocates agree that any reduction in size is likely to be beneficial, not all agree as to what that optimum size should be. In his influential book *The American High School Today* (1959), James Conant stated that a high school serious about preparing students for college needed at least 100 students in its graduating class. This dictum has become the rule of thumb that many people use to come up with a figure of about 400 students for a high school.

Douglas Heath (1994) recommends a range of 200 to 350 students for a lower school, and 400 to 500 students for a high school. Exceeding these ceilings, in his view, increases the potential for unhealthy effects that stem from reduced opportunities for sustained relationships.

> [The school's social climate becomes] impersonal and bureaucratic. Teachers don't know other teachers or students as well as do those in small schools; they don't talk as frequently about individual students or about curricular issues and faculty meetings; and, like students, they do not know who makes what decisions. Students see their friends less frequently, have less contact with adults other than their teachers, participate much less frequently in extracurricular activities, including athletic teams, have much less opportunity to hold leadership positions, are more aggressive and disorderly, and cheat more frequently. Parents no longer visit the school as frequently or know their children's teachers as well [p. 81].

In *A Place Called School*, Goodlad (1984) spoke favorably of the 225- to 250-student size of British Infant School, and mentioned high schools in the neighborhood of 500. He stated, "Indeed, I would not want to face the challenge of justifying a senior, let alone a junior, high school of more than 500 to 600 students (unless I were willing to place arguments for a strong football team ahead of arguments for a good school, which I am not)" (p. 310).

Tom Gregory, whose writings about small schools are consistently thoughtful, regards Goodlad's figure as too high. "The problem with high schools of five-hundred students is that they still function as big schools. It is in this sense that small is too big. High schools of five-hundred students still tend to be governed, though to a diminished degree, by the control issues that dominate big high schools. Many students are still anonymous enough to evade personal responsibility for their actions and therefore cannot be trusted, a fundamental pre-requisite of any school that strives to give students more control over their education, to treat them more as adults" (Gregory, 1992, p. 5).

Gregory's warning reminds us that while size itself is a critical factor in helping schools become communities devoted to caring inquiry and learning, it is not enough. Size provides the required interpersonal setting. Still needed is the cultivation of a social contract or compact that allows the community to speak to principals, parents, teachers, and students with a moral voice. Still needed is a commitment to use what we know about how students learn as we plan curriculum and provide teaching and learning experiences. Still needed is a commitment to teacher development that transforms the faculty into a learning community, and that transforms the school into a center of inquiry. Student learning and teacher development in schools as communities are themes of Chapters Seven and Eight.

Teachers Benefit Too

Students are not the only beneficiaries of "undermanned settings"; teachers benefit as well. And since what is good for teachers usually winds up being good for students, the positive effects multiply. Unfortunately, being large, most schools now wind up with too many teachers. In Gregory's words (1992), "Giving control of schools back to teachers is central to the general improvement of the conditions of teaching. . . . A school that does not work for teachers has little chance of working for students" (p. 6). He agrees with Seymour Sarason's assessment (1990) that good schools are good places for teachers as well as students, but that the sheer scale of things in the typical school gets in the way. Indeed, Gregory's work with Smith (1987) leads him to conclude that as school size increases, the negative effects of having more teachers are felt before the negative effects of having more students. For Gregory (1992), the number of teachers needs to be reduced to a point where everyone can sit around the same table to plan together and to problem-solve together as a group. His suggestion is twelve teachers. With one teacher for every twenty to twenty-five students, we are talking about elementary and high schools of between 240 and 300 students.

If the number of students in the school cannot be reduced directly, schools can be reconfigured into a collection of independent schools within schools or semi-independent houses. A school of 500 students, for example, could function with a lower house of 250 students accommodating first and second year students in either a graded or ungraded environment, and with an upper house for the remaining students. Schools of 1,500 can reconfigure themselves into four or five independent schools or houses.

A strategy for elementary schools is to reconfigure into several families. Instead of grouping all of the first grade classrooms in one corridor, the second grade classrooms in another, and so on, each corridor can contain a first to fifth or sixth grade that functions as an independent family. Students would progress through all of the grades in the same corridor. The metaphor of family fits because such an arrangement enables older children to take responsibility for younger children. They can, for example, take the younger children to the school bus or to the cafeteria, and in other ways look after them. When the fifth graders are ready to "blow their volcano," all of the grades in the family could enter the corridor to watch. Similarly, the second graders would be able to share a play they wrote about Colonial life with the entire school family. A ten o'clock songfest might be scheduled in the corridor each day. The fourth graders might put on a science fair in the corridor inviting each of the other grades to come, to see, to hear, and to share. The first and second grade teachers might decide to join their classes together to function as a multi-aged team. Parents might commit themselves to share crafts, or help with projects and homework every Wednesday afternoon from one to three, thus enabling the five or six teachers in the family to plan together, to share successes, and to learn from each other. Many other configurations for making schools small or intimate learning communities are possible, and most principals and teachers have the necessary skill to invent and implement these new configurations. All they need is the will to change.

But Are Small Schools Cost-Effective?

The conventional wisdom is that bigger schools offer economy of scale that not only increases learning but saves the taxpayers money. Since the turn of the century, our schooling has been modeled after industry-based scientific management principles such as division of labor, specialization, and consolidation, all aimed at making schools more efficient in the use of their human and financial resources. Despite the appeal that this efficiency view has for many policy makers and administrators, the evidence points in the opposite direction. It appears that large schools are actually more expensive to operate, and it appears that small schools are actually less expensive to operate.

Recently the New York City–based Public Education Association and the Architectural League of New York issued three reports examining the feasibility of operating small schools in New York City not as occasional or alternative schools, but as the mainstay of the system.[1] "Small Schools' Operating Costs" concludes:

> The premise that small schools are more expensive to operate has always been false. Research in an educational setting has specifically disproved the economy-of-scale argument at all but a very limited range of school sizes. And *no* research evidence supports the claim that large schools of the size found in New York City (e.g., fifteen-hundred to four-thousand or more) achieve operational-cost-scale efficiencies significant enough to justify their existence or to offset size-related, educationally damaged inefficiencies.
>
> On the contrary, studies show *dis-economies* (penalties) of scale in large schools. Difficult to manage efficiently and safely, large schools require a disproportionate increase in management; an extra "layer" of managers—subject supervisors, assistant-principals,

---

[1] The three publications are: *Schools for New York—Plans and Precedents for Small Schools,* issued by the Architectural League of New York and the Public Education Association, *Small Schools and Savings—Affordable New Construction, Renovation, and Remodelling,* and *Small Schools' Operating Costs—Reversing Assumptions About Economies of Scale,* prepared by the Public Education Association. Copies of all three are available from the Public Education Association, an independent, nonprofit enterprise working since 1895 for better public education in New York City.

deans, additional secretaries—separates principals and teachers [*Small Schools' Operating Costs,* Executive Summary].

As a result of their research, which included an analysis of staffing costs, the investigators identified a number of school organizational factors that could reduce costs:

- reduced or reoriented roles for middle management, most notably assistant principals for supervision;

- more efficient use, with consequent proportionate reduction of clerical staff;

- teacher- and classroom-based guidance;

- cross-teaching and/or teacher-sharing;

- simplified and interdisciplinary curricula;

- reduced need for building security services;

- simplified monitoring;

- cost-efficient multischool sites and houses (*Small Schools' Operating Costs,* Executive Summary).

Relying on the views of experts in the construction industry in estimating school planning, site selection, and other costs, *Small Schools and Savings* concludes that it is possible to build schools as small as four hundred seats at a cost competitive with large school construction. "New Schools for New York" provides drawings and technical details of fifty-two teams of architects and designers showing what cost-effective small schools might look like. Even more savings are anticipated by remodeling existing buildings, or adopting existing nonschool buildings for school use.

Tom Gregory points out that a key savings to small schools is a lower "student/nonteacher" ratio. In his words:

I recall a conversation many years ago with the principal of a large Wisconsin high school. The conversation turned to this ratio. I asked him to estimate how many people were on the payroll in his school, but never taught a class. After accounting for administrators, secretaries, counselors, security guards, nurses, cafeteria workers, and custodians, the total exceeded fifty. In that high school of 1,800 students, the student/nonteacher ratio was about thirty-six to one. The average annual salary of those fifty people today [1992] would probably approach $25,000.00 making the overhead cost of personnel alone for that school about $1,250,000.00 a year, almost $700.00 per student. What might be added to the education of the teenagers in that school if even half of those resources could be applied to instruction instead of the maintenance of the institution?" [1992, p. 15].

Gregory believes that we would be better off modeling schools on the practices of a cottage industry than on the practices of Xerox Corporation, General Motors, or other *gesellschaft* corporations. To make his point, he uses the following example:

The average per-pupil expenditure in this country, and incidentally, also in Minnesota is now about $5,260.00 per year. Envision a small, highly autonomous school, given that funding level. If the school has two-hundred kids in it, its annual operating budget is about $1,050,000.00. Return 20 percent of that amount—$210,000.00— to a trimmed down central administration for its reduced services, and for bus transportation. Imagine a low student-teacher ratio, say 20:1. Pay your ten teachers well, say an average of $45,000.00 a year (including their fringe benefits). Hire a head teacher, and pay him or her $60,000.00. Find an appropriate building for your program in your community, and rent it for $7,000.00 a month plus another $3,000.00 for utilities. Hire a secretary, a custodian, and a cleaning person at $20,000.00 each. Budget $1,000.00 for supplies for each teacher, and $3,000.00 for the central office. Put aside $10,000.00 to buy books each year, and $20,000.00 for computers and A-V equipment. If the idea of [field] trips is appealing, lease three vans, each at $7,000.00 a year. That's probably enough to cover their maintenance, but include another $3,000.00 just to be sure. Put aside $12,000.00 to subsidize the fuel costs of trips. Now comes the fun: figuring out what to do with the $70,000.00 that has yet to be spent [1992, p. 17].

The point of making schools small is not just to save money. Small schools should be valued because they are better for students and better for teachers. It just so happens that as schools get better, they become "more productive." And productivity divided by cost is the classic determiner of efficiency. Even if small schools were to cost a little more money than large schools, they still would be more efficient if the added costs made them more productive than larger schools. Thus in the long run, they would wind up saving taxpayers money. Consider, for example, Central Park East Elementary School in New York City. The school's first 117 graduates obtained high school diplomas, and attended college at much higher rates than did graduates of other public elementary schools in New York City. According to *Education Week* staffer Deborah Viadero (1994b),

> [Researcher Paul Tainsh] calculated the societal-benefit of Central Park East Elementary students' success, and compared them with similar data for students from East Harlem who graduated from other elementary schools in 1983.
>
> He found that the per capita cost of educating students at Central Park Elementary were no higher than they were on average for the entire district.
>
> Moreover, because ten years later more of these students had high school diplomas or were attending college, they could expect to earn $624,000.00 more than their peers over the course of their working careers . . .

As we think about the benefits of small schools, we can learn a great deal from the experience of Catholic schools (and other independent schools). Like many public schools, many Catholic schools serve students from privileged families and circumstances. Some Catholic schools are choosy about who they let in, but so are the public schools in, for example, Sudbury, Massachusetts and Highland Park, Texas. An awful lot of both public and Catholic schools serve children of the underclass, and are not all that choosy about who they let in. Nearly any school can be successful in advantaged situations, but I am impressed with how well many Catholic schools are doing in our inner cities, and in other unlikely places. They seem to be surprisingly successful even though they have fewer professionals, less money, and more modest facilities to work with than do public schools.

There are of course differences between the two systems. For example, parents choose to send their children to Catholic schools, most of which are smaller than their public school counterparts. Nearly all Catholic schools are able to let parents of students know what is expected of them, and to make these expectations stick. Instead of complaining about the differences, maybe we should copy some of them, and in addition, where we can, see if we can invent some unique advantages of our own. We might, for example, pay heed to what Mary Rivera has to say. Rivera is a staunch advocate of public schools, and a former public school principal who now happens to be principal of a Catholic school in West Lynn, Oregon.

> When is someone in public education going to ask the sociological WHY [we find so many successful Catholic schools in unlikely places]?
>
> Are the kids smarter? No. Are their parents wealthier? Higher socio-economically? No. Is it their ethnic background that predisposes academic success? No. Teachers better qualified? Better paid? A resounding NO. Is it religion that makes them study harder? No, certainly not. Did their parent groups care more? Maybe, since they go to great efforts to keep kids in parochial schools. Some other fringe factor?
>
> The key is the strong sense of community.
>
> Parochial schools are smaller, and don't follow the theory that larger is more efficient when it comes to education. Children do not do well in factory-style systems at any age, just as adults don't do well when de-humanized. The fundamental difference in parochial schools is that they are K-8 schools (sometimes with pre-school too) that keep families in the same place for a very, very long time. The people in them feel personal ties. The parents know all the teachers, and the administrators, and those professionals know the whole family. . . . Public schools used to be community/neighborhood-based all grades. They *were* the center of neighborhood life. Everyone knew everyone. Even now, notice the uproar every time a district redistributes kids to schools, or implements some busing plan that's supposed to improve education for someone. Add in the fact that families move several times during a child's elementary years, and add in school transitions required by districts. Add in multi-track plans, which may look like money-savers on paper, but which end up alienating kids and parents and save nothing. That approach doesn't build community or support for schools; it is psychologically destructive [Rivera, 1994].

John Convey's review (1991) of the research on Catholic schools and community confirms Rivera's experiences. He points out that in *The Catholic High School: A National Portrait* (1985), Yeager, Benson, Guerra, and Manno found that 87 percent of the high school principals they surveyed regarded the building of community as one of their top seven educational goals. More principals ranked this goal first or second than any other goal, and 72 percent ranked their schools quite good or outstanding in building community among the students and staff. In addition, Convey cites *Sharing the Faith: The Beliefs and Values of Catholic High School Teachers* (Benson and Guerra, 1985), where over two-thirds of the teachers rated the promotion of the sense of community 'extremely important' or 'very important'" (p. 16).

He cites the research of Bryk and Driscoll (1988) that compared Catholic and public high schools on an index of community they developed. Catholic schools on average had higher scores. The core components of community Bryk and Driscoll found were a system of shared and understood values; rituals, activities, and symbols that signify membership in the school; and a pattern of social relationships that communicated an ethic of caring.

Much of the advantage of Catholic schools can be attributed to size. In San Antonio, for example, thirty-three Catholic elementary schools serve 11,171 students. They range in size from 64 to 694 students, with a median of 318 and a mean of 339. By contrast, the sixty-six public elementary schools in the San Antonio Independent School District serve 33,028 students. They range in size from 21 to 904 students, with a median of 504 and a mean of 500. Similarly, San Antonio's nine Catholic high schools serve 3,235 students. They range in size from 144 to 556 students, with a median of 421 and a mean of 359. San Antonio Independent School District's eight public high schools serve 13,854 students. They range in size from 1,249 to 2,264 students, with a median of 1,645 and a mean of 1,732. In smaller schools, it is easier to develop and nurture the core components of community. It is easier to bring together the kind of consensus and commitment that speaks to everyone in a moral voice.

Underneath this discussion lurks a haunting question. If small schools and small classroom settings are good for students and teachers, good for our pocketbooks, and good for improving student performance, why do we continue our present course of operating existing large schools, and why do we continue to build new large schools? Perhaps it is because we need these large schools to confirm the *gesellschaft* theories of leadership, management, and organization that now dominate school administration. Without large schools, for example, there would be no need for elaborate administrative structures and hierarchies. The roles of assistant principals would have to be reevaluated. Fewer middle managers would be needed between principals and teachers. Custodial requirements would be simplified. Counseling and social work functions would be less formalized. Committing to smaller schools would require us to make some tough decisions about our present resource and personnel allocation policies. But in the end, parents, students, and teachers would be better served. Small size is a tough choice, but it is also the right choice because it helps us to see the small picture better. And, as Miami teacher Nancy Webster (1994) points out below, it is the small picture that counts big for students:

> "You just don't see the big picture, Nancy," said my exasperated principal. She was absolutely right, of course. I'm a pre-kindergarten teacher in the public schools, an early-childhood professional who inhabits a tiny piece of the "Education World." My frame is young children in a large elementary school (approximately 1,500 students), in a very large school system.

> This really BIG picture is full of problems I know but can't fix and vocabulary I understand but can't use: competency-based curriculum, authentic assessment, CORE, Total Quality Management, whole language, and a lot of other words. My work begins the process of schooling. A teacher for 25 years, I've seen the vocabulary change, the classes get larger, the programs come and go, and more children fail. Meanwhile, "at risk" children have entered our vocabulary, along with "dysfunctional families." The BIG picture is full of schedules, time constraints, pull-out programs, team meetings, computer-assisted grades, and paperwork. It's the modern elementary school at work.

> My little world, on the other hand, is 4-year-olds learning to control themselves, trying to get along with each other, expressing themselves in many ways, and gathering information about the world. It's pretty simple: no workbooks, just learning through doing,

developing skills, and, with any luck, having fun doing it. It's a world of blocks, crayons, books, paint, dolls, and small cars. It involves people, art supplies, and basic equipment. My conversation with my principal, in fact, involved a playground, a place where active, big-muscle-oriented 4-year-olds could practice climbing, sliding, hanging, balancing, and moving. That's a major part of any day for young children.

My class loves coming to school. Parents tell me the children miss it on weekends. They come in smiling, greet their friends, make plans, and start playing at a chosen center of activity. They're learning to share (cooperative learning?), mastering small-muscle skills by cutting with scissors, building with blocks, sticking counting pegs in boards (competency-based curriculum?), proudly showing me their pictures and art projects (authentic assessment?), singing "Mother Goose" rhymes (CORE?) while they move their fingers across the page (whole language?). This doesn't need fancy rhetoric, lots of meetings and paperwork; only trained people who care, who can observe and clarify, who can be a positive role model, who possess lots of patience, a sense of humor, and an energy level Batman would envy. . . .

Schools with over a thousand elementary students are big business. Thus, the emphasis on T.Q.M., a system big business uses to mange and build "quality."

It's too bad, really, because schooling is essentially about teaching, learning, and young people. It's small . . . simple . . . and focused, when done well [p. 52].

Chapter Seven

Doing What's Best for Students

Form should follow function. School decisions should be based on what we believe is good, and on what we know is effective for enhancing student academic, social, and moral development. But too often our imported theories of schooling provide us with ready-made forms for organizing, developing curriculum, planning for teaching and learning, providing for teacher development, and for making other school decisions. With form already in place, our job is then to figure out how we can craft goals and develop strategies that fit. Function follows form.

Students who play high school football in well-designed programs and under progressive leadership, for example, can learn a great deal about sportsmanship, leadership, community, and responsibility. They often get important self-esteem boosts, and they benefit physically as well. Further, their grades are usually better, and they are likely to be better behaved. But our present forms of competition in high school allow only about one hundred students to get these benefits. Whether we like it or not, the other fourteen hundred students in a fifteen-hundred-student high school have to settle for being spectators.

If we started with the form-should-follow-function premise that opportunities for sportsmanship, leadership, community, responsibility, increased self-esteem, physical development, and improved grades should be widely available to students, then we would have to develop sports programs that are quite different from those we now have in the typical American high school. Our fifteen-hundred-student high school, for example, might decide that it needs to field five teams in order to accommodate students' interests and talents. If this school were to join with three other high schools, each fielding five teams, they would have formed a twenty-team league with two divisions. Imagine a "super-bowl" play-off for the champions of the two divisions. What fun this would be for the players, students, spectators, and parents. And think of all the football talent that would be discovered as more students who want to play, and have some talent for the game, get to play when form follows function.

As a further example, most parents and teachers probably agree with the statement "teachers need to know students well in order to teach them well." But our present forms of scheduling classes and organizing the curriculum require us to assign high school teachers six classes and 150 students a day, and then to allow them to spend only fifty minutes at a time with each student. Under these circumstances, knowing students well is difficult—as is teaching them well. But instead of changing this form to fit the desired function of providing more personalized teaching, too often we try to meet caring and personalization goals by doing such things as adding a half-period a day of "advising" to the existing schedule, by creating "at-risk" programs for students who are obviously suffering from the present system, or by introducing other programs without changing the basic forms of scheduling and schooling. Though these add-ons can be helpful, they do not address the basic problems inherent in our present forms of schooling. Function continues to follow form.

Community Theory provides us with an opportunity to create forms that fit better what we want to accomplish. At the center of Community Theory is the principle that leadership and decision making should be idea based. Shared ideas speak to principals, parents, teachers, and students in a moral voice. This voice provides a more powerful and more compelling source of authority for what they do than does bureaucratic or personal leadership—the two sources of authority that are at the center of the Pyramid, Railroad, and High Performance Theories.

The moral authority of idea-based leadership rests on four pillars:

1. The unique shared values that define each individual school as a covenantal community

2. The democratic principles and conceptions of goodness that provided the foundation for the establishment of our republic
3. The findings and insights that educational research tells us are most effective for enhancing the academic, social, and moral development of students
4. The findings and insights that our informed reflection and the informed reflections of others tells us is good for enhancing the academic, social, and moral development of students

As sources of authority, the four pillars provide the basis for making decisions about what to do in schools as communities, and for how to do it. They represent seminal design principles (functions) from which school forms can then be crafted. The first two pillars, the unique values that give each individual school special meaning, and the common democratic and moral values that bring all schools together in a shared political legacy, are themes discussed throughout this book (see, for example, Chapter Four, The Moral Voice of Community). In this chapter, the focus will be on the third and fourth pillars: what research tells us is most effective, and what informed reflection tells us is good for enhancing the academic, social, and moral development of students.

Together they place "doing what's best for students" at the center of decision making. Both research and informed thought point more and more to the constructivist view of teaching and learning as being best for students. This view acknowledges that no one best way to teach can be mandated for all teachers to follow or to use in all situations. Constructivist thinking puts the teacher in the driver's seat as the key decision maker as to what to do, how to do it, and when to do it. Decisions reflect in part personal dispositions, but in the main are driven by purposes, unique teaching and learning contexts, and constructivist principles of learning. Teaching is deliberate in the sense that teachers are able to explain what they are doing and why. Further, they are able to show that their decisions are good for students and effective for different contexts. This chapter summarizes the constructivist view and makes an argument for this view to become the basis for decisions we make about schooling.

School Purposes

Though many lists of school goals and purposes exist, most readers will probably agree that schools should help students to communicate, to know, to think, to be good, and to commit to something. Stated more formally the five purposes of schooling are:

- To develop basic competency in the three R's
- To pass on the culture
- To teach students to think
- To build character
- To cultivate excellence

The first three purposes are widely accepted. It is hard to argue with the idea of transmitting mastery of basic skills and fundamental processes required for thoughtful participation in the economic and civic life of our country and planet, or with promoting the intellectual development of students.

Character development too is typically mentioned in historical and contemporary studies of the goals of education (see for example Goodlad, 1984). But, as James Lemming (1994) points out, by the 1950s character education pretty much disappeared in U.S. schools. It wasn't until the late 1960s that schools became interested again in the topic. For roughly the next twenty years, the emphasis in character education was on teaching youngsters *how to* resolve moral dilemmas, and *how to* clarify their values. In both of these movements, teachers were not to take positions, to teach good and bad or right and wrong, or to otherwise "moralize," but to teach children how to reason and how to value, so they could make their own informed decisions about good and bad and right and wrong. As long as students reasoned properly, teachers were expected to respect the values that students expressed.

In recent years, this relative approach to character education has been de-emphasized somewhat as problems of character are addressed more deliberately and directly. Sex education provides an example. Increased emphasis is given to providing students with comprehensive information that will help them make better decisions about their sexuality. Unfortunately, the new emphasis given to sex education seems to have been unable to achieve the desired results. After reviewing the research, Lemming (1994) observed that sex education programs may provide students with more knowledge about sexuality, but they seem not to change student values or behavior, a conclusion reached as well by Whitehead (1994).

Lemming reports similar findings for drug and alcohol education. He concludes that codes, pledges, and teacher exhortations alone are unlikely to have a lasting effect on character; and further, the development of a student's capacity to reason about moral issues does not seem to result in related changes in behavior. In those few places where Lemming finds character education working, it is less a program added to the curriculum, and more a part of the everyday culture of the school. He notes, for example, "Character develops within the social web or environment. The nature of that environment, the messages that it sends to individuals, and the behaviors it encourages and discourages are important factors to consider in character education" (p. 57).

Both Lemming and Thomas Lickona point out that character education is becoming increasingly popular across the country. Lickona (1993) believes that there are three reasons for this popularity: the decline of the family; the troubling trends in youth character; and the greater acceptance of the belief that—regardless of our diversity—at root we share a basic morality that includes such virtues as responsibility, respect, trustworthiness, fairness, caring, and civic virtue.

In discussing troubling trends in youth character, Lickona points out that the culprit is not just the failure of too many families and communities, but the wrong kind of adult models; the overplaying of sex, violence, and materialism; and the negative pressures of student and other peer subcultures. In his words, "Evidence that this hostile moral environment is taking a toll on youth character can be found in ten troubling trends: rising youth violence; increasing dishonesty (lying, cheating, and stealing); growing disrespect for authority; peer cruelty; a resurgence of bigotry on school campuses from pre-school through higher education; a decline in the work ethic; sexually precocity; a growing self-centeredness and declining civic responsibility; an increase in self-destructive behavior; and ethical illiteracy" (p. 9).

Etzioni (1993, p. 92) defines character as the psychological and moral muscles that allow a person to control impulses and delay gratification. Character develops as students acquire the ability to control impulses and the capacity to do things for reasons other than the satisfaction of biological needs or immediate desires.

Developing character requires more than just introducing character education programs. It requires that schools "look at themselves through a moral lens, and consider how virtually everything that goes on there affects the values and character of students" (Lickona, 1993, p. 10). Lickona believes that this approach to character education calls upon each teacher in a school to:

- *Act as care-giver, model, and mentor,* treating students with love and respect, setting a good example, supporting positive social behavior, and correcting hurtful actions through one-on-one guidance and whole-class discussion;

- *Create a moral community,* helping students know one another as persons, respect and care about one another, and feel valued membership in and responsibility to, the group;

- *Practice moral discipline,* using the creation and enforcement of rules as opportunities to foster moral reasoning, voluntary compliance with rules, and a respect for others;

- *Create a democratic classroom environment* involving students in decision making and the responsibility for making the class a good place to be and learn;

- *Teach values through the curriculum,* using the ethically rich content of academic subjects (such as literature, history, and science), as well as outstanding programs[1] . . . as vehicles for teaching values and examining moral questions;

- *Use cooperative learning* to develop students' appreciation of others, perspective taking, and ability to work with others toward common goals;

- *Developing the "conscience of craft"* by fostering students' apprecia-

---

[1] See, for example, *Facing History and Ourselves,* a holocaust curriculum for eighth graders available from the Facing History and Ourselves Foundation, 25 Kennard Road, Brookline, MA 02146, and the Character Education Curriculum available from the Character Education Institute, 8918 Tesoro Drive, San Antonio, TX 78217.

tion of learning, capacity for hard work, commitment to excellence, and sense of work as affecting the lives of others;

- *Encourage moral reflection* through reading, research, essay, writing, journal keeping, discussion, and debate;

- *Teach conflict resolution,* so that students require the essential moral skills of solving conflicts fairly and without force [Lickona, 1993, p. 10].

A comprehensive approach to character education is more likely to occur in schools that are more *gemeinschaft* than *gesellschaft. Gemeinschaft* schools provide that social web or environment that his review of the literature reveals is so important to the development of character. In Lemming's words:

> Since the development of character involves the acceptance of norms valued by the community as binding on the individual, organizations characterized by *gemeinschaft* are more ideally suited for the task of character education. Belonging to a *gemeinschaft* means essentially belonging to a moral community, and living up to such norms as sharing, self-sacrifice, and collective responsibility. The individual in such social organizations values the quality of relationships, and shares a concern with others for appropriate behavior; one attempts to become a valued member of the normative community to maintain these significant relationships. . . . When the conditions of community are created in classrooms or schools, . . . these [character education] programs are more effective at developing character than the more common school setting [p. 56].

Students, it appears, learn virtue by being around virtuous people and by being part of social networks that represent webs of meaning with moral overtones.

Cultivating Excellence

The fifth purpose of schooling cited above, *to cultivate excellence by having students commit to something,* also needs explaining. Following Mindy Kornhaber and Howard Gardner (1993) we might define excellence as regular, high-level performance in "domains of knowledge" that are considered to be important. A domain of knowledge consists of facts, principles, and skills that have evolved over time because they are useful in sustaining a particular culture's economic or social needs.

Kornhaber and Gardner's view of excellence is much wider than the traditional view usually attributed to *gesellschaft* schools. In the traditional view, excellence in schools is thought to relate to high class rank, top test scores, and the winning of academic awards that reward persistence and brilliance in linguistic and logical-mathematical learning—the domains that are considered to be at the foundation of the traditional subjects taught in school. *Linguistic* refers to the ability to use words effectively either orally or in writing. *Logical-mathematical* refers to the ability to use numbers effectively, and to reason well.

In his seminal book *Frames of Mind* (1983, 1985) Howard Gardner views linguistic and logical-mathematical abilities as only two of seven different intelligences. To him, an intelligence is "the ability to solve problems, or to create products that are of value within one or more cultural settings" (1985, p. x). But not all problems lend themselves to being solved by applications of linguistic and logical-mathematical ability. And not all products valued in a given culture require linguistic and logical-mathematical ability for their creation. Architects, interior designers, artists, and inventors, for example, solve important problems and create important products by relying less on linguistic and logical-mathematic abilities, and more on spatial abilities or *spatial intelligence* (the ability to perceive the visual-spatial world accurately). Similarly, athletes, dancers, mechanics, and surgeons may well need to be competent in the linguistic and logical-mathematical functioning, but their excellence depends on highly developed *bodily kinesthetic intelligence* (the ability to use one's body to express ideas, and one's hands to create or transform things).

Gardner identifies three other unique competencies for a total of seven that comprise his theory of multiple intelligences. The other three are *musical, interpersonal,* and *intrapersonal intelligence.* (Interpersonal intelligence refers to the ability to perceive and value others; intrapersonal intelligence refers to the ability to know oneself and to adapt one's behavior accordingly.)

Gardner (1989) believes that "While it is theoretically possible that an individual could excel in all intelligences, or perform at the same level in all intelligences, both of these outcomes would be empirically rare. In most cases, individuals exhibit a fairly jagged profile of intelligences, revealing relative strengths in some areas, comparative weaknesses in others. The theory also posits that these different profiles can be detected early in life and that, while they are not immutable, it is probably prudent to go with the grain rather than wholly against it" (pp. 150–151).

In more simple language, people are smart in different ways. Their unique abilities help them to contribute differently, but still valuably, to solve problems and to create things that are important to people. For example, consider "Kimberly," a student at the Key School in Indianapolis. Kimberly is required to develop projects to share with teachers and others as evidence of what she has learned.

> Kimberly's projects usually entail a drama or dance performance. One was an extended and well-rehearsed balletic dance to contemporary, popular music. In another she researched and rehearsed a variety of dances that were in vogue during this century. She then performed the dances to music appropriate to their respective eras. Alongside this, she created a poster of drawings showing fashions that were worn during each decade of the century. For the "Heritage" theme, we watched her deliver from memory an expressive dramatic monologue based on the experience of a slave girl.

> In nearly all her projects, Kimberly demonstrates excellence by giving skillful performances on challenging assignments in disciplines that are widely appreciated in the larger society. Her achievement is not surprising given her talent and her delight in and dedication to dance and drama as well as the support she receives both at home and in school for her efforts. Nor is it surprising that Kimberly was subsequently admitted to a magnet school for the arts based on her dance and drama auditions. What may be more surprising, is that this school success comes in the face of marginal results on [traditional] IQ tests, and a failing grade on the state's standardized test of math and English [Kornhaber and Gardner, pp. 1–2].

Striving to cultivate excellence by having each student commit to something, work at it, and master it to a standard of excellence makes sense in part because, like adults, students have different talents, interests, and capacities. Cultivating excellence recognizes the reality that in the adult world of work and play distinguished performance counts the most, brings the greatest personal rewards, and contributes the most to the common good.

Cultivating student talents to a standard of excellence is an important and effective strategy for helping them to develop basic competencies in other capacities and in other dimensions of intelligence. As Kornhaber and Gardner (1993) point out,

> Kimberly's teachers at the Key School would engage her interpersonal, bodily kinesthetic, and spatial intelligences to grapple with diverse areas of curriculum. We saw inklings of Kimberly's willingness to exploit her competencies in the area of history with her exploration of changes in costume, music, and dance, which drew her into library research. These same intelligences and interests can be used to strengthen her language skills as well. Kimberly's teacher could encourage her to write her own dramatic monologues, or have her conduct interviews with performing artists, and write up what she has learned. Given her interests and profile of strength, it is possible to envision ways of making a unit on the body truly intriguing for this child. How do muscles develop? Why does exercise make a difference? What other systems does the body rely on to maintain health and strength? Physical sciences might be broached through topics like acoustics and lighting that coincide with her interest in stagecraft. How does sound carry to the back of the audience? How do so many different colors come out of just the few gels that cover the stage lights?" [p. 14].

Learning to do something special and do it well is not only good for students and good for society, it is also a practical solution to the problem of "knowledge explosion." It is becoming increasingly difficult for schools to try to cover a "well-balanced curriculum." Trying to master everything often results in mastering nothing. As Gardner (1989) points out, "In light of the proliferation of disciplines and sub-disciplines, and the discovery of diverse products and values from the many cultures of the world, a different state of affairs has begun to prevail during the past century. However reluctantly, we have all come to realize that the ideal of universal knowledge (or even of universal knowledge ability) is no longer tenable. The renowned mathematician John von Neumann put it trenchantly when he noted that a century ago it was possible to understand all of mathematics, but by 1950, even the most well-informed mathematician could have access to only 10 percent of the knowledge of his field" (pp. 148–149).

How do schools provide the kind of coverage of the world's knowledge that is needed, but not do it superficially? One solution to this problem is to sample the spectrum of the disciplines by teaching the exemplars of history, literature, science, and so on. Some exemplars would need to be standard for schools across the country to reflect our common heritage and destiny or to reflect the fundamental structures of a particular discipline such as biology. But most exemplars might be chosen to reflect the particular purposes, values, and cultural nuances that comprise the essence of a particular school community.

Choosing to study only a few things, but studying them well, is a strategy that makes sense if it is combined with a commitment to help students to learn how to think, to research, to inquire, to learn on their own. This combination of depth of knowledge with a capacity for and commitment to lifelong learning makes particular sense when combined with a commitment to help each child to become excellent in something. Gardner (1989), for example, believes "that each individual should know well at least one or two domains of knowledge; have a sense of the range of those domains he or she cannot personally come to know in detail; be cognizant of significant perspectives and alternatives in the realms of truth, beauty, and goodness; and have the skills and the inclination to think about the important issues in life, ranging from his or her personal role and relation to the immediate family, to engagement with the wider community, to his or her niche in the world" (p. 153).

The Constructivist Approach

Constructivist teaching and learning brings together the five purposes of schooling: helping students to communicate effectively, to know, to think, to be good, and to commit to something by learning to do it well. Central to constructivist thinking is the transformation of classrooms and schools into learning communities.

Community provides the integrating focus for pursuing the purposes in such a way that each reinforces the other.

Learning requires knowledge, which comes in many forms.[2] Sometimes knowledge is limited, and at other times knowledge is generative. *Limited knowledge* does not lead anywhere, but is simply accumulated, stored, and recalled. *Generative knowledge,* by contrast, leads to more learning, new learning, more expansive learning, and the transfer of learning. Generative knowledge is used to create new knowledge. It is the kind of knowledge that can be used to help students understand new situations, to solve unfamiliar problems, to think, to reason, and to continue to learn. Before knowledge becomes generative for students, they must elaborate and question what they have learned, they must be able to examine new information in relationship to other information, and they must build new structures of knowledge.

Some constructivists make still another distinction between *declarative knowledge* and *procedural knowledge.* This distinction is helpful in understanding what generative knowledge is and how the two purposes, "helping students to know" and "helping students to think" can be brought together in a way that each reinforces the other. Declarative knowledge refers to subject-matter content, and procedural knowledge refers to processes such as how we think, how we solve problems, and how we synthesize. Whether declarative knowledge turns out to be limited or generative depends on how content and thinking skills are taught. Are the two taught separately, or taught together? If they are taught separately, it is not likely that the curriculum will emphasize teaching students to become lifelong learners. Subject matter provides the substance and context for developing problem solving and reasoning. And without meaningful subject matter, attempts to teach problem solving and reasoning become gamelike, and even trivial.

Constructivists emphasize teaching subject matter for understanding, and emphasize using subject matter in the real world. Again the two purposes reinforce each other. It is easier to teach for understanding if the context is the real world, and real-world

---

[2] This discussion of constructivist theory and research follows that which appears in *The Principalship: A Reflective Practice Perspective,* 3rd ed. (Sergiovanni, 1995, pp. 189–192).

applications require meaningful understanding. Emphasizing the two requires that students be involved in the construction of knowledge. This means not just telling and explaining, but providing students with opportunities to answer questions, to discuss and debate meanings and implications, and to engage in problem solving in real contexts. According to Brophy (1992):

> Early in the process, the teacher assumes most of the responsibility for structuring and managing learning activities and provides students with a great deal of information, explanation, modelling and cuing. As students develop expertise, however, they can begin regulating their own learning by asking questions and by working on increasingly complex applications with increasing degrees of autonomy. The teacher still provides task simplification, coaching, and other "scaffolding" needed to assist students with challenges that they are not ready to handle on their own. Gradually, this assistance is reduced in response to gradual increases in student readiness to engage in self-regulated learning [p. 6].

Relying on the research of Anderson (1989) and Prawat (1989), as well as his own work, Brophy (1992) identifies the following principles of good subject-matter teaching:

1. The curriculum is designed to equip students with knowledge, skills, values, and dispositions useful both inside and outside of school.
2. Instructional goals underscore developing student expertise within an application context and with emphasis on conceptual understanding and self-regulated use of skills.
3. The curriculum balances breadth with depth by addressing limited content but developing this content sufficiently to foster understanding.
4. The content is organized around a limited set of powerful ideas (key understandings, and principles).
5. The teacher's role is not just to present information but also to scaffold and respond to students' learning.
6. The students' role is not just to absorb or copy but to actively make sense and construct meaning.
7. Activities and assignments feature authentic tasks that call for problem solving or critical thinking, not just memory or reproduction.

8. Higher-order thinking skills are not taught as a separate skill curriculum. Instead, they are developed in the process of teaching subject-matter knowledge within application contexts that call for students to relate what they are learning to their lives outside of school by thinking critically or creatively about it or by using it to solve problems or make decisions.
9. The teacher creates a social environment in the classroom that could be described as a learning community where dialogue promotes understanding [p. 6].

Many of the principles that Brophy provides are part of other research traditions as well. Two, however, are particularly unique to the constructivist perspective. One is the importance of helping the classroom become a social community, and the other is the importance of learning through engagement in real work. Constructivists point out that social relationships are key in the process of learning, and that as classrooms become learning communities and communities of inquiry, social relationships enhance individual and group learning, and the processes of learning and inquiry cement further feelings of community. Much of the new research, for example, points to the value of cooperative living and learning within the classroom as being key, not only for the benefits it provides with respect to "helping students be good," but with respect to "helping students know" and "helping students think" as well.

In a learning community, knowledge exists as something that is both individually owned and community owned at the same time. The two feed off each other. A particular student's own individual growth and accumulated knowledge contributes to the shared growth and accumulated knowledge that exists in the classroom as a whole. And in turn, as this accumulated knowledge expands, so does individual knowledge.

Constructivists emphasize the importance of relating new learning to prior knowledge, and the importance of immersing teaching in the world of "authentic" learning. Learning is always contextual. What is learned depends on one's prior knowledge, on the social context for learning, and on the connections between what is being learned and the real world.

Sometimes a student's prior knowledge interferes with learning or encourages the student to learn the wrong things. Students often bring misconceptions or naive theories and notions to their studies. Linking new ideas to prior knowledge that is wrong may result in the further accumulation of faulty learning. This problem is more likely to be noticed and more likely to be taken care of in personalized learning settings that acknowledge the social nature of learning. These settings allow teachers to get up close, to understand where students are coming from. The importance of authentic learning, and the provision of "cognitive apprenticeships" or excursions into the real world to promote authentic learning cannot be overestimated. Students learn best by doing, and doing is best when it involves engagement with real or near-real problem solving. Effective learning settings allow learners to use shared knowledge to solve problems, and allow students to practice their skills in real-life settings.

Summing the Principles

From the constructivist research come a number of principles that are strikingly simple yet powerful:

Not all subject-matter content is equal in teaching for understanding. The most powerful subject matter is generative, and generative subject matter should dominate the curriculum. Generative subject matter is central to the disciplines from which it comes, is accessible to students, and can be connected meaningfully to other important topics both inside and outside of the discipline in question (Perkins and Blythe, 1994).

Less is more. It is important to cover less subject matter, but to cover it well. Students need to repeat key experiences, to observe and reobserve events, and to think and rethink as a way to build deeper understanding.

Combining process with substance is unbeatable. The most powerful learning opportunities exist when challenging and interesting subject matter is taught in a context that helps students learn how to think, how to solve problems, and how to learn for themselves.

Project planning and teaching is better than lesson planning and teaching. Project planning and teaching involves students in an in-depth investigation of disciplinary and interdisciplinary problems. Such problems require careful study of issues, histories, theories, and other kinds of subject matter. Students master rigorous subject-matter content, problem solving, and research skills while they also develop, practice, and expand such basic communication skills as reading, writing, and other symbolic forms of representation.

Students are more producers of knowledge than they are consumers, much as we may prefer otherwise. What students learn does not automatically follow from what they are taught. Lessons taught are always mediated by the values and experiences that students bring to teaching, and by the unique meanings they attribute to what is taught.

Teaching and learning must be personalized so that teachers are able to help with this construction of knowledge. Teachers must know how to listen to students—and have the time and interest to do so–in order to encourage this construction while providing the needed guidance and structure.

The best indicator of what a student knows is the work itself. The work of students is important, and should comprise a record to be revisited by teachers and students, a record to be used for further teaching and assessment, and a record to be shared with parents.

An important aspect of teaching for understanding is setting up social norms that promote respect for other people's ideas (Lampert, cited in Brandt, 1994). These norms encourage the ethic of learning, and the sharing of ideas.

The aim of teaching is to provide the conditions for learning. Simply delivering concepts, facts, and ideas to students is secondary. Providing the conditions involves active planning and participation, joint inquiry, and above all being an active organizer and promoter of learning occasions. "We must be able to catch the ball that the children throw to us, and toss it back to them in a way that makes the children want to continue the game [of learning] with us, developing, perhaps, other games as we go along" (Fillipinni, 1990, cited in Edwards, 1993, p. 153).

The Importance of Personal Meanings

Most of the constructivist principles can be brought together around the importance of personal meanings. The personal meanings that students bring to every learning encounter act as filters through which all learnings are processed. Culturally defined meanings are important, as well. These are the meanings that others hold for learners. Teachers, for example, often have specific expectations for what students should learn when they read a particular book or when they are exposed to a particular lesson. Communities and societies too have clear sets of expectations for the meanings that students should extract from many of the learning experiences that they encounter in schools. Still, culturally defined meanings can never be completely separated from personal meanings. Indeed, as constructivist thinking implies, it is when students are able to understand things not only as they are, but in terms of their own personal contexts, that learning is maximized. Consider the following example:

> A group of youngsters is asked to write an essay or report describing the homes, people, and traffic patterns they observed from the bus window returning home to the suburbs from a field trip to a pier in a nearby city. The teacher expects them to compare these observations with their own community as part of a social studies unit on neighborhoods. Jimmy, who lived many years in a brownstone much like hundreds of others passed in a crowded neighborhood of a nearby city, might write an essay quite different from those of his new suburban classmates. Indeed, his rich and warm version of the urban neighborhood, the alley, the corner candy store, the hot nights spent sleeping on the roof under the stars, stick ball, Italian ices, and the feelings of comradeship in sitting on the stoop with his family and friends could help him wind up with a poor paper if it were judged according to the objectives and fact-oriented comparative criteria set forth by the teacher. The word "neighborhood" has a culturally defined meaning, but for Jimmy this meaning would be colored and enriched by his own personal experiences [Sergiovanni and Elliott, 1975, p. 43].

The noted curriculum theorist James B. Macdonald (1964) believes that the integration of both personal and culturally defined meanings are important not only in learning, but for healthy psychological development as well. In his words:

> The self is not "actualized" in a vacuum, but in a world. The world is, however, primarily as it is perceived by the self. For the world to become only what one feels it is, is to retreat into psychosis; but for the world to be accepted only as it is defined, in terms of rational, cultural knowledge, is certainly a form of neurosis. In neither case is the ego integrated into a functional, open, and reality-oriented structure.

> It should be apparent to all that the growing self must have per-
> sonal meanings and cultural meanings for adequate realization.
> Further, it follows from this, that the two meanings systems are not
> separate compartments within the individual. They are (in a
> healthy state) functionally integrated into the purposeful striving
> of the person [p. 39].

Thirty-five years ago, Arthur W. Combs (1959) criticized the
neglect of personal meaning in school as follows:

> In our zeal to be scientific and objective, we have sometimes taught
> children that personal meanings are things you leave at the school
> house door. Sometimes, I fear, in our desire to help people learn,
> we have said to the child, "Alice, I am not interested in what you
> think or what you believe. What are the facts?" As a consequence,
> we may have taught children that personal meanings have no place
> in the classroom, which is another way of saying that school is con-
> cerned only with things that do not matter! If learning, however, is
> a discovery of personal meaning, then the facts with which we must
> be concerned are the beliefs, feelings, understandings, convictions,
> doubts, fears, likes, and dislikes of the pupil—those personal ways
> of perceiving himself and the world he lives in [p. 11].

The constructivists hope to correct this problem by pointing
out that students are producers of knowledge, and what they produce is very much influenced by the personal meanings that they
bring to their learning experiences.

Getting the Models Right

Models and examples are useful learning devices. They provide us
with frames and images that can help us to think more clearly about
our problems, and to invent solutions. But too often, our models
and examples have provided us with the wrong frames and images.
As Lilian Katz (1993) points out,

> In the U.S. the principal models and metaphors used—especially
> at the primary and secondary school levels—come from the indus-
> trial and corporate world and its factories rather than from the ex-
> tended family or communal life. Nursery schools were developed

from nurseries that were places in the home devoted to the nour-
ishment and care of the very young. However, during the last
twenty years or so, the term "nursery" in the U.S. literature related
to programs for three-to-five-year-olds has been completely
replaced by the term "pre-school"—as in pre-cooked and pre-
shrunk. . . . Concepts frequently used in educational discussion,
such as delivery systems, cost-benefit ratios, pre-specified specific
behavioral learning outcomes, outcome-based curriculum, curricular packages, packaging of innovations, teacher-proof materials, the
child-care industry, and so on, portray the application of the industrial model to the design, operation, and assessment of schooling
[pp. 33–34].

By contrast, the constructivist approach is based on a "home-
grown" set of ideas that emerge from school research, and that
clearly apply to school settings. Do constructivist models exist in
practice? Yes, many. The Key School in Indianapolis, Indiana; Central Park East Secondary School in New York City; the Jackson Keller
Elementary School and the International High School of the Amer-
icas in San Antonio; and hundreds of other public and private
schools across the U.S. and Canadian landscapes serve as models.

The theme of this chapter is that doing what is best for students
should be the basis for the decisions we make about schooling. Compelling evidence exists that the constructivist view of teaching and
learning should be central. If we are serious about following the rule
"form should follow function," then the constructivist view and the
school purposes it supports should be the standard for making decisions. Community Theory helps by providing the intellectual framework for accomplishing this goal. But little will be accomplished for
students over the long run unless the same constructivist standards
and the same community standards are applied as well to teachers—
the theme of the next chapter.

Chapter Eight

Teacher Development and Schools as Centers of Inquiry

There is growing acceptance of the idea that general improvements in student performance will occur only when classrooms become learning communities, and teaching becomes more learner centered. The state of Texas, for example, recently adopted a set of proficiencies for teachers aimed at creating "learner-centered schools." Included in this document are such ideals as:

> The teacher is a leader of a learner-centered community, in which an atmosphere of trust and openness produces a stimulating exchange of ideas and mutual respect. The teacher is a critical thinker, and problem solver who plays a variety of roles when teaching. As a coach, the teacher observes, evaluates, and changes direction and strategies whenever necessary. As a facilitator, the teacher helps students link ideas in the content areas to familiar ideas, to prior experiences, and to relevant problems. As a manager, the teacher effectively acquires, allocates, and conserves resources. By encouraging self-directed learning, and by modelling respectful behavior, the teacher effectively manages the learning environment so that optimal learning occurs [Texas Education Agency, 1994, p. 4].

The kind of teaching and learning needed to create learning communities envisioned above can significantly enhance student academic, social, and moral development. But any serious attempt to provide for it in Texas or anywhere else must include as its strategy the transformation of classrooms into:

Reflective Communities within which students develop insights into their own strength and weaknesses as learners, and use this information to call upon different strategies for learning.

Developmental Communities within which it is acknowledged that students develop at different rates, and at any given time are more ready to learn some things than others.

Diverse Communities within which different talents and interests of students are not only recognized, but acknowledged by decisions that teachers make about curriculum, teaching, and assessment.

Conversational Communities within which high priority is given to creating an active discourse that involves the exchange of values and ideas among students, and between students and teachers as they learn together.

Caring Communities within which students not only learn to be kind to each other and to respect each other, but to help each other to grow as learners and as persons.

Responsible Communities within which students come to view themselves as part of a social web of meanings and responsibilities to which they feel a moral obligation to embody in their present behavior as students, and future behavior as citizens.

It is not likely that we will be successful in transforming our classrooms into communities of this kind unless we are able to transform our schools similarly. Few axioms are more fundamental than the one that acknowledges the link between what happens to teachers and what happens to students. Inquiring classrooms, for example, are not likely to flourish in schools where inquiry among teachers is discouraged. A commitment to problem solving is difficult to instill in students who are taught by teachers for whom problem solving is not allowed. Where there is little discourse among teachers, discourse among students will be harder to promote and maintain. And the idea of making classrooms into learning communities for students will remain more rhetoric than real unless schools become learning communities for teachers too. Thus for classrooms to be transformed, schools themselves must be transformed into:

Professional Communities within which "learning and teaching
depend heavily upon creating, sustaining, and expanding a
community of research practice. Members of the community
are critically dependent on each other. . . . collaborative learning is not just nice but necessary for survival. This interdependence promotes an atmosphere of joint responsibility, mutual
respect, and a sense of personal and group identity" (Brown,
1994, p. 10).

Improving schools involves identifying the right leverage points
for change. Our present theories of school leadership and organization, unfortunately, point us in the direction of school
improvement strategies that too often miscalculate which leverage
points for change are high, and which leverage points are low. The
Pyramid and Railroad Theories, for example, rely on instituting
management systems of one kind or another, and on mandating
specific actions and programs. The High Performance Theory
emphasizes the provision of inducements in the form of material
and psychological rewards to get people to improve. In this theory,
motivating teachers and inspiring teachers to perform by exchanging rewards for compliance is the key.

But as McDonnell and Elmore (1987) point out, two other policy instruments are available to leverage school improvement—
"capacity-building" and "systems-changing." Capacity-building
involves enabling and empowering teachers by increasing their
skills, and increasing their commitment to professional values. Systems-changing involves changing our basic theories of schooling
in ways that allow for a new sense of what is effective and what is
good practice, and a new distribution of authority. Understanding
change differently, as when we switch the metaphor for the school
from organization to community, is an example of systems-change.
And placing teacher development at the center of our school
improvement strategies is an example of capacity-building. Teacher
development as capacity-building is the theme of this chapter; we
will take up systems-change in the next chapter.

Many years ago, Vito Perrone (1978) pointed out that the
teacher's role is central to improving the quality of learning for students. For him, teacher development is key because "The quality of
teachers' understandings influences to a large degree what teach-

ers do in classrooms" (p. 298). Good teacher development programs and efforts, he reasoned, should be based on the assumption that "The best source for teachers to learn more about teaching and learning, child growth and development, materials and methods is through an examination of one's own practice" (p. 298).

More recently, Milbrey McLaughlin has pointed out that key to teacher learning is for teachers to be empowered in ways that enable and allow them to exercise more control over their classrooms. She believes that this control is needed for teachers to make the changes in their practice that are necessary for them to teach more effectively (cited in Bradley, 1993). Her research with Joan Talbert revealed that teachers' participation in a professional community of like-minded colleagues had a powerful effect on their ability to know better what to do in the classroom, and to adopt their teaching strategies to more effectively meet students' needs. Where such collegiality is high, teachers have more positive views of teaching, and teach more successfully (McLaughlin and Talbert, 1993).

Lichtenstein, McLaughlin, and Knudsen (1992) believe that professional knowledge plays a central role in empowering teachers. They point out that "the 'knowledge' that empowers teachers is not the stuff of the weekend workshop or the after-school inservice session. The knowledge that empowers teachers to pursue their craft with confidence, enthusiasm, and authority is knowledge of the teaching profession, in the broadest possible sense" (pp. 40–41). The researchers were able to identify three overlapping sources of professional knowledge: knowledge of professional community, knowledge of educational policy, and knowledge of subject matter. Knowledge of educational policy and knowledge of subject matter were strengthened as teachers participated in professional organizations and other networks of teachers. Particularly key was knowledge of professional community—the array of developmental experiences that teachers accumulate as a result of working collaboratively with other teachers in a shared practice. Knowledge of professional community empowers teachers by helping them recognize their own expertise, and by expanding their "notions of what is possible in their own practice and the profession as a whole" (p. 43).

Can professional community help teachers to learn to teach for understanding? McLaughlin and Talbert think so. They observed that "some teachers who attempted such changes in practice . . . were unable to sustain them and became frustrated and discouraged. This is because learning how to teach for understanding goes against the grain of traditional classroom practice and so entails radical change and risks obstruction. Those teachers who made effective adaptations to today's students had one thing in common: each belonged to an active professional community which encouraged and enabled them to transform their teaching" (1993, p. 7).

If teacher development is to become a natural part of building professional community and if teacher development is to move to center stage in the school improvement process, then schools need to create the kinds of management and supervisory systems, organizational patterns, and teacher growth strategies that:

- Encourage teachers to reflect on their own practice
- Acknowledge that teachers develop at different rates, and that at any given time are more ready to learn some things than others
- Acknowledge that teachers have different talents and interests
- Give high priority to conversation and dialogue among teachers
- Provide for collaborative learning among teachers
- Emphasize caring relationships and felt interdependencies
- Call upon teachers to respond morally to their work
- View teachers as supervisors of learning communities

Viewing teachers as supervisors of learning communities provides them with a new identity that has implications not only for their roles in the classroom, but for teacher development as well. As Marilyn Evans (1994) points out, "The premise is that if teachers are to build learning communities in their classrooms, they must first experience being part of a learning community" (p. 4).

Models of Teacher Development

Traditionally, teacher development has been synonymous with inservice training. And inservice training methods have emphasized such pedagogical principles as uniformity, consumption, memorization, and replication. Schools carefully develop (or purchase carefully developed) and present training programs for teachers. Teachers are then given practice in using the training they receive. There is usually some follow-up in the form of supervision to make sure that the training takes. In recent years, the emphasis has been switched from training to professional development and, with the advent of constructivist thinking, to renewal as ways to think about teacher development.[1] Table 8.1 describes and contrasts the training, professional development, and renewal approaches.

All three approaches have important roles to play but not all approaches should receive the same emphasis. If we value teaching for understanding, the development of thinking, and other constructivist principles of teaching and learning, then we need to give less attention to training models and more attention to professional development and renewal models.

Training approaches to teacher development resemble traditional in-service programs that are well known to teachers and principals and need little elaboration. They are best suited when a problem can be defined as teachers not knowing about something or needing to improve their skills in some area. Training is linked to clear objectives and relies on conventional, well-executed instruction. Teachers, for example, might be introduced to various ways in which interest centers can be set up, methods for evaluating student portfolios, new techniques for using simulation for teaching world history, tips on monitoring student progress, or some basic teaching skills that help keep students "on task." Teachers generally assume passive roles. Techniques most often used are oral presentations, illustrated presentations, demonstrations, and observations of good practice. Effective training programs provide opportunities for teachers to practice what they learn and then to receive coaching as they actually begin to use the new material in their classrooms.

Although training has its place, most observers believe that it should no longer be the primary model for teacher development.

---

[1] This discussion of approaches to teacher development is drawn from "Teacher Development and Supervision," a chapter in *The Principalship: A Reflective Practice Perspective,* 3rd ed. (Sergiovanni, 1995, pp. 208–211).

Table 8.1. Approaches to Teacher Development.

	Training	Professional	Renewal
Assumptions	Knowledge stands above the teacher.	The teacher stands above knowledge.	Knowledge is in the teacher.
	Knowledge is, therefore, instrumental. It tells the teacher what to do.	Knowledge is, therefore, conceptual. It informs the teacher's decisions.	Knowledge is, therefore, personal. It connects teachers to themselves and others.
	Teaching is a job and teachers are technicians.	Teaching is a profession and teachers are experts.	Teaching is a calling and teachers are servants.
	Mastery of skills is important.	Development of expertise is important.	Development of personal and professional self is important.
Roles	Teacher is consumer of knowledge.	Teacher is constructor of knowledge.	Teacher is internalizer of knowledge.
	Principal is expert.	Principal is colleague.	Principal is friend.
Practices	Emphasize technical competence.	Emphasize clinical competence.	Emphasize personal and critical competencies.
	Build individual teacher's skills.	Build professional community.	Build a caring community.
	Through training and practice.	Through problem solving and inquiry.	Through reflection and reevaluation.
	By planning and delivering training.	By emphasizing inquiry, problem solving, and research.	By encouraging reflection, conversation, and discourse.

Source: Sergiovanni, 1995, p. 209.

Implementing lists of do's and don'ts, standard skill repertoires, and other scripts is not the way to help teachers to teach for understanding, to develop student thinking, and to promote generative knowledge. Instead, teachers need to learn how to think on their feet, inventing their practice as they go.

The relationship between teachers and the knowledge base for teaching is understood differently in professional development than in training. Professional development assumes that teachers are superordinate to the research on teaching. Unlike technicians who are trained to apply research findings, professionals view research as knowledge that informs the decisions they make. Professionals create their practice in use. For them, the process of inquiry and the practice of their profession are inseparable.

Professional development approaches emphasize providing teachers with a rich environment filled with teaching materials, media, books, and devices. With encouragement and support, teachers interact with this environment *and with each other* through exploration and discovery. Judith Warren Little (1993) proposes six principles she believes should guide the design of professional development experiences for teachers.

1. Professional development offers meaningful intellectual, social and emotional engagement with ideas, with materials, and with colleagues both in and out of teaching.
2. Professional development takes explicit account of the context of teaching and the experience of teachers. Focused study groups, teacher collaboratives, long-term partnerships, and similar models of professional development afford teachers a means of locating new ideas in relation to their individual and institutional histories, practices, and circumstances.
3. Professional development offers support for informed dissent. In the pursuit of good schools, consensus may prove to be an overstated virtue. . . . dissent places a premium on the evaluation of alternatives and the close scrutiny of underlying assumptions.
4. Professional development places classroom practice in the larger context of school practice and the educational careers of children. It is grounded in a big-picture perspective on the purposes and practices of schooling, providing teachers with a means of seeing and acting upon the connections among students' experience, teachers' classroom practice, and school-wide structures and cultures.

5. Professional development prepares teachers (as well as students and their parents) to employ the techniques and perspectives or inquiry. . . . it acknowledges that the existing
knowledge is relatively slim and that our strength may derive
less from teachers' willingness to consume research knowledge
than from their capacity to generate knowledge and to assess
the knowledge claimed by others.
6. The governance of professional development ensures bureaucratic restraint and a balance between the interest of individuals and the interests of institutions [pp. 138–139].

Little offers the principles as alternatives to training models
that, when used excessively, provide teachers with shallow and
fragmented content and subject them to passive roles as they participate in scripted workshops. She believes that the principles
are antidotes to the "one-size-fits-all" problem that training too
often presents. Further, she argues that the principles challenge
the view that teaching is a narrowly defined technical activity. Little believes that today's emphasis on teacher inservice education
is dominated by "a district-subsidized marketplace of formal programs over which teachers exert little influence or in which they
play few leadership roles" (p. 139). In professional development
models, the teacher's capacities, needs, and interests are central.
Teachers are actively involved in contributing data and information, solving problems, and analyzing. Principals are involved as
colleagues. Together, principals and teachers work to develop a
common purpose themed to the improvement of teaching and
learning. Together, principals and teachers work to build a learning and inquiring community.

Both training and professional development approaches share
the purpose of helping teachers to improve their practice. Frances
Bolin, Judith Falk, and their colleagues (1987) point out that
although this kind of improvement may be a legitimate goal, it is
not powerful enough to tap the potential for teachers to grow personally and professionally. Bolin (1987) asks:

What would happen if we set aside the question of how to improve
the teacher and looked instead at what we can do to encourage the
teacher? . . . asking how to encourage the teacher places the work
of improvement in the hands of the teacher. It presupposes that

the teacher desires to grow, to be self-defining, and to engage in teaching as a vital part of life, rather than as unrelated employment. This leads to looking at teaching as a commitment or calling, a vocation . . . that is not adequately contained in the term profession as it has come to be used. [p. 11]

Bolin believes that when the emphasis shifts from improving to encouraging, both training and professional development give way to renewal. In her view, renewal is not driven so much by professional problems as by a teacher's commitment to teaching as a vocation. Renewal implies doing over again, revising, making new, restoring, reestablishing, and revaluing as teachers individually and collectively reflect on not only their practice but themselves and the practice of teaching that they share in the school.

In training, the emphasis is on building each individual's teaching skills by planning and delivering instruction. In development, the emphasis is on building professional community by helping teachers to become inquirers, problem solvers, and researchers of their own practice. In renewal, the emphasis is on building a caring community by encouraging teachers to reflect and to engage in conversation and discourse.

The School as an Inquiring Community

Chapter Seven made the case for classrooms to become learning, caring, and inquiring communities. This chapter argues that it is difficult to create such classrooms unless the school itself becomes a place where learning, caring, and inquiring among teachers is common. These virtues are the ingredients needed for schools to become professional communities. Key to community in both classrooms and schools is a commitment to inquiry, and a commitment to learning as the basis for decisions about structure, organization, sources of authority, curriculum, teaching methods, assessment, and other school issues.

Several models exist that can help us create learning and inquiring communities. But not all models will be equally helpful. The literature on "learning organizations," for example, has many useful ideas that stimulate us to think creatively about this issue. This literature seems particularly appropriate for applying to large educational systems. Many big elementary and secondary schools and big school districts would qualify. Senge (1990), for example, points out that the literature on learning organizations can help leaders become better systems thinkers.

> Systems thinking is a discipline for seeing wholes. It is a framework for seeing interrelationships rather than things, for seeing patterns of change rather than static "snapshots." It is a set of general principles—distilled over the course of the twentieth century, spanning fields as diverse as the physical and social sciences, engineering, and management. It is also a set of specific tools and techniques, originating in two threads: in "feedback" concepts of cybernetics and in "servo-mechanism" engineering theory dating back to the nineteenth century. During the last thirty years, these tools have been applied to understand a wide range of corporate, urban, regional, economic, political, ecological, and even physiological systems. And systems thinking is a sensibility—for the subtle interconnectedness that gives living systems their unique character. . . . All around us are examples of "systemic breakdowns"—problems such as global warming, ozone depletion, the international drug trade, and the U.S. trade and budget deficits—problems that have no simple local cause. Similarly, organizations break down, despite individual brilliance and innovative products, because they are unable to pull their diverse functions and talents into a productive whole [pp. 68–69].

But from a practical standpoint, the characteristics of "learning organizations" are difficult to apply to small family and community-oriented schools in a meaningful way. Much of this literature was developed with *gesellschaft* business organizations in mind. Single and double loop learning, complex systems diagrams, and other structural-functional ideas just don't fit *gemeinschaft* families, churches, and schools very well.

Lieberman and Miller (1986) have observed that the most promising school improvement strategies place their emphasis on the teacher, the classroom, and the patterns of interaction that exist among teachers and between administrators and teachers in the school. In their words:

> Whether we look at local problem-solving, research transformed into practice, action research, or networking, we were drawn to the

teachers, their world, and their work as the starting point for improving schools.

What, then, are our new understandings about staff development and school improvement?. . . . what we have rediscovered are some tried and true notions that have become enriched and expanded over time. Among them:

- Working *with* people rather than working *on* people.

- Recognizing the complexity and craft nature of the teacher's work.

- Understanding that there are unique cultural differences in each school and how these affect development efforts.

- Providing time to learn.

- Building collaboration and cooperation, involving the provisions for people to do things together, talking together, sharing concerns.

- Starting where people are, not where you are.

- Making private knowledge public, by being sensitive to the effects of teacher isolation and the power of trial and error.

- Resisting simplistic solutions to complex problems; getting comfortable with reworking issues and finding enhanced understanding and enlightenment.

- Appreciating that there are many variations of development efforts; there is no one best way.

- Using knowledge as a way of helping people grow rather than pointing up their deficits.

- Supporting development efforts by protecting ideas, announcing expectations, making provisions for necessary resources.

- Sharing leadership functions as a team, so that people can provide complementary skills and get experience in role taking.

- Organizing development efforts around a particular focus.

- Understanding that content and process are both essential, that you cannot have one without the other.

- Being aware of and sensitive to the differences in the worlds of teachers and other actors within or outside of the school setting [pp. 108–109].

Teacher development is a key theme in the ideas they present. Thankfully, we have models of our own to help us build the kind of professional community we want for teachers and the kind of learning community we need for students.

The compelling literature on adult learning represents a rich source of ideas worth considering. The United Theological Seminary (UTS) in Dayton, Ohio, for example, relies on this literature in organizing and implementing its Doctor of Ministry program. UTS students assume responsibility not only for organizing their academic work, but for creating and giving leadership to a community of learners they are responsible for assembling. The members of this community supervise the student's work and guide the student through the preparation of the dissertation. UTS faculty, consultant faculty from other universities, and other persons whom the student and her or his advisor think will be helpful, join the student as members of this learning community. Mary Olson views the doctoral program as an andragogical model of adult continuing education in which:

1. Persons can and should be empowered to become self-reliant learners who are no longer dependent on "institutional settings" for their continuing education. The program affirms the belief that persons can assume responsibility for their own learning needs from within their own contexts of active ministry. While others can help, the primary responsibility for learning must be accepted by the learning persons.
2. Learning should be a process of praxis and reflection, taking place in the context of living. According to this principle praxis and reflection are not two separate moments in the learning process, related only by a rhythm of involvement and withdrawal, with praxis taking place "in the field" and reflection in the classroom. Rather, praxis and reflection are viewed as integral to every moment of learning.
3. Form should follow function in the learning process. The identification of learning needs and interests should determine the structure and content of learning and should precede the development of any learning "program."
4. Learning takes place in community. While the individual must take responsibility for one's own learning, the spirit of mutual inquiry is basic to the andragogical approach to education. All perceptions are tested by the perceptions of others and the learner must be open to the fullest range of such perception.

5. Learning best takes place as a perpetual movement of discovery and invention. Persons learn when they discover things for themselves rather than when someone else determines what they ought to know. What others can do is to raise questions, present issues, and create situations which stimulate and require such discovery [United Theological Seminary, 1994, p. ii].

These same principles can be used to design teacher development programs on the one hand and to provide the environment, structures, and resources that can help teachers accept responsibility for their own development on the other.

The School as Center of Inquiry

Another model worth considering is the concept of *school as center of inquiry* proposed by Robert J. Schaefer twenty-seven years ago (1967). His basic proposal was that we create a new teaching profession comprised of scholar-researchers and scholar-practitioners who would become students of their own teaching practice and front-line researchers of the complex problems of school learning. His vision was the transformation of teaching from a technical occupation of skilled doers to a profession of skilled thinkers. For this to happen, he reasoned, the school itself must be converted from a distribution center for knowledge to a producer of knowledge. In Schaefer's words, "We can no longer afford to conceive of the schools simply as distribution centers for dispensing cultural orientations, information, and knowledge developed by other social units. The complexities of teaching and learning in formal classrooms have become so formidable and the intellectual demands upon the systems so enormous that the school must be much more than a place of instruction. It must be a center of inquiry—a producer as well as a transmitter of knowledge" (p. 1).

Why should the school become a center of inquiry? Schaefer offered three reasons that remain as compelling today as they did then. First, though we know a lot more than we ever did about teaching and learning, there is much we simply do not know. Even as the knowledge base expands, no one best way will exist that can be applied uniformly and effectively to all students. Good teaching requires that teachers reflect on their practice, and create knowledge in use as they analyze problems, size up situations, and make decisions.

Teachers, then, must become researchers of their practice and inquirers into their profession. One critical difference between teacher as technician and teacher as professional is that the technician is subordinate to the knowledge base of teaching. In this image, teacher education programs and in-service staff development programs are designed to train teachers to apply this knowledge in practice. The teacher as professional, however, is superordinate to the knowledge base of teaching. This knowledge does not tell the teacher what to do, but informs the decisions that the teacher makes about what to do.

The second reason that Schaefer gave for his vision of the school as a center of inquiry was that such a change would keep teachers alive intellectually. "It is not only our need for new knowledge, but also our responsibility for the intellectual health of teachers which suggests that schools should be conceived as centers of inquiry. When divorced from appropriate scholarship in substance and in pedagogy, teaching resembles employment as an educational sales clerk and ceases to be a more than humdrum job. . . . By concentrating upon the distributive function alone, the school effectively imprisons rather than liberates the full power of the teacher's mind" (Schaefer, p. 2). The implications of students being taught by teachers whose minds have been "imprisoned" as opposed to "liberated" are not very pleasant.

The third reason that Schaefer gave for his vision of the school as center of inquiry was a pragmatic one. If our aim is to help students become lifelong learners by cultivating a spirit of inquiry and the capacity for inquiry, then we must provide the same conditions for teachers—a theme that runs throughout this chapter.

Schaefer did not believe that the patterns of school organization he observed could sustain the kind of scholar-practitioner that he envisioned for teachers to be. Things have not changed much during the last twenty-seven years, as researchers Lortie (1975), Johnson (1990), and Lieberman and Miller (1984) so painfully reveal. Schools still tend to be organized as dispensaries rather than as places where issues are raised and inquiry takes place.

Teaching as dispensary evokes simple and routine rather than strong and intellectual images of the teaching profession. These images encourage the presumption that teachers must teach students all day, a situation that leaves little or no time for reflection, research, or in-depth conversation with colleagues. Unlike physicians and lawyers, who spend only a portion of their time conferring with clients,

> The teacher is ordinarily too pressed for time to meditate upon his successes or, for that matter, his failures. The hours which are not consumed in personal interactions are at least partially devoted to clerical and administrative routines, such as keeping attendance, organizing collections, maintaining records for report cards or principals, and mimeographing materials. For even the moderately conscientious person this schedule is lengthened by the necessity of using evenings and weekends for lesson planning, correcting papers, and completing similar chores. It is difficult to imagine that our affluent society would condone such a work load if it conceived of teaching as something other than the routine transmission of elementary information [Schaefer, p. 36].

Instead of being dispensers of knowledge, teachers—like physicians, lawyers, architects, and other professionals—must become producers of knowledge. Professionals transmit and dispense, but at root their job is to produce something worth transmitting or dispensing in the first place. Professionals create knowledge in use as they practice.

Not only will it be necessary to change technical metaphors of teaching to professional ones, the workday itself must be rethought to find the time for teachers to reflect and to invent together as they learn and teach together in a shared practice. But this kind of configuration will not be possible unless more superintendents, principals, and other administrators are willing to put aside the existing system of executive authority, and to replace it with collegial authority—an authority embedded in shared commitments, shared ideals, and professional responsibility. Teachers too must step forward and support such a change by expressing a willingness to accept more responsibility for what goes on in the school.

Replacing executive with collegial authority will not be easy for three reasons:

- Our present system is hampered by a lack of faith.
- Many administrators are afraid they will lose power.

- Many teachers are unwilling to accept their share of the burdens of leadership.

At their roots, our present theories of schooling are based on a lack of confidence in the capacity of people to respond. As Christopher Jenks points out:

> The school board has no faith in the central administration, the central administration has no faith in the principals, the principals have no faith in the teachers, and the teachers have no faith in the students. . . . In such a system it seems natural not to give the principal of a school control over his budget, not to give the teachers control over their syllabus, and not to give the students control over anything. Distrust is the order of the day, symbolized by . . . the time clocks . . . the constant tests, and elaborate regulations for students [Jenks, 1965, cited in Schaefer, 1967, p. 40].

Distrust results in part from fear that any redistribution of power that benefits teacher, parents, or student will result in losses to school boards and administrators. Despite solid research to the contrary, many administrators believe that the distribution of power in a school is a concept governed by zero-sum economic laws. There is a fixed pie of power that equals 100 percent. If you give away 40 percent to teachers, you only have 60 percent left. Give another 20 percent away to parents, and you are stuck with only 40 percent. How can a principal run a school with only 40 percent of the power? The research of Arnold Tannenbaum (1968), however, reveals a different picture. He found that leaders can actually increase control by giving up power. Sharing power actually means more power for everyone. *Power has the capacity to expand.* His research reveals that the total amount of power and influence that exists in an enterprise across different ranks is a better predictor of satisfaction and performance than is the relative amount of power and influence held by any one group as compared with another.

A few years ago, I had the opportunity to address a group of teachers who had won awards for being among the most talented and best performers in their respective schools. Toward the end of my remarks, I asked two questions: Who in your school is in the best position to "supervise and evaluate" you? And, would you be willing to accept responsibility for "supervising and evaluating" your peers? Predictably, the answers were as follows: "The teacher next door and the teacher across the way are in the best position to evaluate me." Principals and supervisors were clear losers in this contest. And "No, I do not feel it is my place to supervise and evaluate my colleagues, it's the principal's job." The reality that many teachers are reluctant to accept more responsibility for what goes on in schools, even with administrator encouragement, is a vexing problem. Too many teachers have been urged to expand before only to be "burned" in the end. The concept of school as center of inquiry may help in resolving this problem. Teachers would not be asked to adopt a new behavior or new responsibilities within the old cultural context of the school, but would be asked to help reconstruct the culture itself.

Schaefer concluded his argument for the need to transform schools into centers of inquiry by noting that "Major structural changes would be required in school organization to create centers of inquiry, to free the scholar-teacher from crushing teaching burdens, to establish appropriate collegial associations, to provide the necessary facilities for study, and to establish and maintain fruitful relationships with universities" (p. 77). The theories of leadership that we have borrowed from other fields do not shed much light on these issues. A community theory of schooling, by contrast, can address these issues squarely. The question for us is, "Are we up to it?" Do we believe enough in "doing what's best for students" that we are willing to create the right conditions for teachers on whom we depend for so much? Are we willing to not just espouse the principle "form should follow function," but to struggle to make it a reality? Are we willing to make decisions and create school designs that help teachers develop personally and professionally, and that make it easier for them to engage students in meaningful teaching and learning?

Besides the moral question of doing what is best for students, there is a practical question that must be considered. The school is and will likely remain the center of change. Sirotnik (1989) notes, for example, that not only are schools the targets of educational improvements, but they are the sources of improvements (or lack of improvements) as well. Despite reports of national commissions, despite state mandates, and despite carefully engineered and expertly driven change strategies, it is the 2.2 million teachers that account for 26 billion teacher-student contact hours in schools across the nation that will in the end decide what happens to students. In Sirotnik's words, "That the centers for educational change and school improvement are anywhere else than in the nation's schools, would be a difficult proposition to defend in light of these statistics" (p. 89). This is the reality that makes emphasizing teacher development and school as center of inquiry so compelling.

Chapter Nine

A New Theory of Change

The "capacity-building" teacher development discussed in the previous chapter is essential but not sufficient; it won't "take" well in a cultural vacuum. We also need to engage in serious "systems-changing" that will lead us to a new and different understanding of the change process, and allow schools to grow into learning communities.

What does change mean for us as individuals and for the schools we serve? Why is change in schools so hard to implement? How do we do it? How do we make changes stick once they are implemented? Is change always good, or should we resist a lot of it? There are no easy answers to these questions about educational change. A lot depends on our mindscapes of schools. Different mindscapes will produce different answers, even contradictory answers, to the same questions.

Mindscapes, as argued in Chapter One, function as practical theories that influence what we see, what we believe, what issues we consider important, and ultimately what we do. They operate much like perception pictures. Imagine, for example, several children looking at that famous picture of the vase formed by two profiles. Some of the children will see the vase, but not the profiles. Others will see the profiles, but not the vase. It would be difficult for the children to share stories about what they saw. The image that each child experiences provides a mindscape that creates a different reality.

Similarly, our realities about change issues and the change strategies we choose are a function of our mindscapes of schools. When our change strategies do not work, we are prone to think that the problem is with our choices. So, we search the same mindscapes again looking for still another strategy to try. Rarely do we consider the possibility that our mindscapes may be wrong. And until we do, it is likely that change will remain a vexing issue for all of us. We need mindscapes of schools, for example, that deinstitutionalize the responsibility for change and that lessen the necessity for formal occasions for change, so that both become part of the everyday life of teachers and principals as they practice together.

Let me share a personal example. At one time I held the view that schools were organized and operated much like the mechanical workings of a windup clock. I acquired this "structural-functional" view of schools by studying organizational theory and the traditional management sciences, paying particular attention to how the ideas from these disciplines were successfully applied to businesses, transportation systems, and other *gesellschaft* enterprises. The image for me was one of cogs and gears that represented different dimensions of the school's organizational structure—each with a specific function, and each connected to every other function in a grand, rational, linear system.

Within this clockwork view of schools, I believed that school leaders were supposed to work hard to improve things by introducing changes that got control of the main gear and pin. They were, of course, not to be dictatorial or mean-spirited in this effort. I believed that effective leaders practiced enlightened human-relations leadership that was sensitive to the needs of teachers and others, and that would then motivate them to accept and implement the desired changes. Once the main gears and pins were under control, then all the other wheels and pins could be expected to move in predictable and reliable ways according to one's plans. The leader's intents would then be accomplished, and schools would get better. This rational and linear view of leadership and change was based on four principles:

- Schools are managerially tight, but culturally loose. Thus what matters most are the change systems that are introduced and not the norm systems that exist in the school.
- Systematic and detailed planning is important to achieve the needed clarity, control, and consensus for change to work.
- When fitting people into the planning-for-change process, first emphasize ends, then ways, and finally means.

- Incentives and disincentives are necessary to motivate people to change (Sergiovanni, 1989, 1991).

When Linear Theory Meets the Real World

In reality, none of the principles hold up very well. Although they seem logical and persuasive because they agree so well with the current mindscape, the current school *landscape* is another matter entirely.

But Schools Are Managerially Loose and Culturally Tight

Far from being managerially tight and culturally loose, real schools look more like clockworks gone awry. The cogs and pins are there alright, but they spin independently of each other. We have, for example, teacher evaluation systems that are designed to help teachers teach in approved ways. But in reality, they are typically nonevents. Site-based management changes some things in the school, but seems not to affect what goes on in classrooms. The curriculum that students receive is closer to the one that is in the minds and hearts of teachers than the one that is mandated by the central office. What teachers are told to do and trained to do during Friday's in-service might be seen in Monday's classrooms during the principal's walk-through, but not after.

Like police officers and other street-level bureaucrats, teachers—and principals, too—acknowledge the existence of mandates, directives, supervisors' preferences, school rules and regulations. In practice, they often "show boat" what needs to be done to comply with requirements when necessary. But for the most part they ignore many requirements, bend others, and invent still others with impunity to fit the situations they face (Lipsky, 1980; Morris, Crowson, Porter-Gehrie, and Hurwitz, 1984). Going for the main gear and pin by relying on management approaches to change may look good, sound sensible, and seem very rational, but *over time* this strategy produces no appreciable changes. Sure, we can point to TQM, MBO, flexible scheduling, the lesson cycle, the school effectiveness correlates, and other often-helpful innovations that have been implemented. But few remain in place for very long. It appears that teachers are less influenced by management strategies, and more influenced by what they believe, by what peers believe and do, and by other and more elusive cultural matters.

In 1976, Karl Weick popularized the idea that schools are managerially loose but culturally tight. He referred to schools as being "loosely coupled systems." In such systems, according to Weick (1976) "shared premises, culture, persistence, clan control, improvisation, memory, and imitation" (p. 10) count more and have more effective influence than do strategies that rely on detailing job specifications, engineering work flow, creating management protocols that tightly align various school functions together, or introducing other related structural changes. In his words:

> In a loosely coupled system you don't influence less, you influence differently. The administrator . . . has the difficult task of affecting perceptions, and monitoring and reinforcing the language people use to create and coordinate what they are doing. . . . Administrators model the kind of behavior they desire . . . identify key issues so they can centralize control over a few (not all) issues and help people see them similarly. Leaders in loosely coupled systems have to move around, meet people face-to-face and to do their influencing by interaction rather than by rules and regulations. . . . Personnel selection is more critical than in other systems, because the common premises that are selected into that system will guide how the dispersed activities are executed [p. 10].

But Systematic and Detailed Planning Can Backfire

Within the clockworks mindscape, systematic and detailed planning for change is accepted as a given. Clarity, consensus, and control are thought to be impossible without such planning. Planning for change is supposed to unfold as follows:

- Decide what it is that you want to accomplish, and if possible, state it as a measurable outcome.
- Provide clear behavioral expectations to people by deciding and communicating who will do what, and how it will be done.
- Train people to function in the new way.
- Once the change is introduced, monitor by comparing what you expected with what you observed.
- Make any corrections in the system that may be necessary.

This approach to planning for change is a variation of leaders having visions and then arranging events and people in ways that make their visions a reality. It makes sense in a linear and stable world, but not in schools where the majority of human interactions and events that take place are nonlinear.

Planning for change provides us with a number of paradoxes. By planning in a linear way, we assume that it is possible to control the future. But in reality, we often lose control as a result of the plan. Detailed plans can take over from people, becoming scripts that program their future actions, and becoming self-fulfilling prophesies that determine their destiny even when they may no longer be interested in that destiny.

Further, detailed planning has a tendency to result in the "escalation of commitment" to a course of action that sustains itself irrationally long after it should have been abandoned (Staw, 1984). For example, commitment to a teacher-evaluation system that took many hours of planning time to develop is likely to remain firm even when the evidence indicates that the teaching effectiveness research on which the system is based is faulty, or that teacher morale is suffering as a result. Ambitious building projects for expensive state-of-the-art school facilities designed to accommodate large numbers of students are likely to be completed—and repeated—even in the face of compelling evidence that simpler and smaller school designs are better for students. After sacrificing the amount of time, money, and effort in career planning and development needed to become an educational administrator in today's *gesellschaft* schools, administrators are likely to resist changes that upset the existing hierarchical equilibrium even if the changes make sense for teachers, parents, and students.

And finally, though traditional planning is intended to increase the likelihood that desired school improvements will be implemented, unanticipated consequences often produce opposite effects. The key to traditional planning, for example, is to encourage consistency between what it is we *want* to implement and what it is we *do* implement. But by stating intents in detail beforehand, too many worthwhile outcomes not stated or unanticipated don't count. Too many new priorities and new courses of action can be missed. Thus in the long run, innovation may be discouraged.

Even corporations are feeling the effects of the unanticipated consequences of detailed planning. The well-known management consultant Tom Peters (1989b) points out that firms without central planners tend to get better results than those that have central planners. He believes that a better strategy is to organize and plan as we go along, utilizing the best talents of people to respond to the idiosyncratic nature of situations as they arise.

The importance of achieving clarity, control, and consensus remains important. But how can we achieve these in planning for change and still be successful? The community perspective suggests that we need to be clear about the basic direction of schools by setting the overall tone. Leaders can do this by providing the kind of purposing that invites teachers, parents, and students to help forge a covenant, a moral compact, that includes shared goals, values, and standards in the form of operating principles. Included in this compact would be a commitment that everyone should be held accountable for embodying the ideas in the compact. Being committed to shared goals and becoming self-managing, it appears, are viable substitutes for detailed planning. How much planning is needed in this approach? Just enough to set the "compass" direction, and not enough to provide mandatory "road maps." Let schools, principals, and teachers develop their own maps. Let the process of planning unfold as they go along.

But Means-Ways-Ends Strategies Work Better

The issue of where to fit people into the planning-for-change process bears on the discussion above. The traditional ends- ways- means approach resembles the firing of a cannon. Cannons are great for hitting fixed targets. First you identify your target. Then you carefully aim your cannon. And finally, you give your disciplined crew the order to fire. But in schools, most of our targets are constantly moving, and more desirable targets often appear during the course of our actions. A cannon approach just doesn't work for us. Harry Quadracci (cited in Peters, 1989a) has suggested that if we have to use a target-hitting metaphor, a cruise missile approach makes more sense. Cruise missiles have the built-in capacity to chase moving targets. And they have the built-in capacity to change their targets in midair.

In effect, as argued in Chapter Two, we need to invert the traditional ends, ways, and means approach. We need to start with means by building up the capacity of people to become self-managing, and by helping people connect to shared values and ideas. This approach emphasizes the development of a *shared followership* in the school—a followership that includes principals, teachers, parents, and students. Robert Kelly (1988) believes that being self-managing is an important hallmark of being a good follower. Followers, he points out, share these characteristics:

- They manage themselves well.

- They are committed to the organization and to a purpose, principle, or person outside themselves.

- They build up their confidence and focus their efforts for maximum impact.

- They are courageous, honest, and credible [p. 144].

Being a good follower requires more than being committed to do what is necessary. One must know *how* to do it; competence is important as well. Once a self-managing shared followership begins to emerge in the school, then people should be encouraged and helped to figure out for themselves what to do and how to do it. Odds are that the decisions they make and the goals and objectives they achieve will be consistent with shared purposes.

But Incentives and Disincentives Can Hinder

It is commonly assumed that extrinsic incentives and disincentives are necessary to motivate people to change. Stated more candidly, "If you want to get people to do something, you have to give them something they want in return." This is a variation of the motivational rule "what gets rewarded gets done." But unfortunately, once we begin to rely on this rule in schools, its flip side becomes true too. What does not get rewarded does not get done. Relying on rewards to motivate people to change leads to calculated involvement. As long as desired incentives are provided, you have a good chance of getting people to go along with proposed changes. But once incentives are not available, or no longer desired, then cooperation will be harder to get.

A more serious problem with "what gets rewarded gets done" is the displacement of connections. Once people are provided with incentives to do something, the reasons why they do this thing can change. Consider, for example, incentive systems for children that often turn play into work (Greene and Lepper, 1974). Students might be engaged in a learning activity because of its intrinsic interest. No gold stars, certificates, tokens, or other external rewards are provided for their involvement. But once these extrinsic rewards are introduced, the students' connection to the activity has a tendency to change from intrinsic to extrinsic. If the rewards are then taken completely away, students are not likely to engage in the activity again (Greene and Lepper, 1974, Deci and Ryan, 1985).

Similarly, teachers who are engaged in certain kinds of activities because they feel a sense of obligation or believe that something is right or important to do are likely to forsake this moral involvement for a calculated one, once incentives or disincentives are introduced. In short, calculated involvement seems able to get teachers and students to do what they are supposed to as long as rewards are forthcoming. But calculated involvement does not provide connections that are powerful enough to inspire and motivate people to work without direction or supervision, or to remain engaged in their work when extrinsic rewards are not available.

In addition to "what gets rewarded gets done," change strategies need also to give attention to "what is rewarding gets done," and "what is good gets done." The two latter rules recognize the importance of intrinsic motivation on the one hand, and the human tendency to respond to morality, emotions, and social bonds (Etzioni, 1988, p. xii) on the other. The evidence suggests that teachers and students are more likely to engage in long-term effort when they find their activities intellectually challenging and significant than when they have extrinsic reasons for their participation (see, for example, Herzberg, 1966; Kohn, 1986).

Beyond intrinsic factors, what counts most to people is what they believe, how they feel, and the shared norms and cultural messages that emerge from the groups and communities with which they identify. As Etzioni (1988) reminds us, human beings pass moral judgments over their urges. "For example, people save not merely to consume in their old age, but also because they believe it is indecent to become dependent on the government or on their children. And people pay taxes not merely because they fear the penalties, but also because they consider their government to be a legitimate institution" (p. x). Parents and teachers routinely sacrifice their own self-interests, wants, and needs to advance those of the children they have responsibility for raising. And both define what needs to be done in raising children within a web of meaning constructed of norms from groups with whom they identify. Table 9.1 summarizes the three motivational rules and their implications.

Replacing Rules-Based with Norms-Based Strategies

It is a truism that schools must change continually to keep up with changes in their environment. But are there ways in which conditions might be created for this kind of continual change to occur naturally? Or must we view the process of change as something someone must do to others? Instead of thinking about change as an artifact of a strategy, management plan, or other grand scheme, can the culture of the school be reconstituted in such a way that change becomes as natural as breathing? Is it possible to shift the lion's share of responsibility for providing leadership for change away from hierarchies, and give this responsibility to individuals as

Table 9.1. Rules of Motivation.

The Rules	Why People Behave	How They Are Involved
What gets rewarded gets done.	Extrinsic reasons.	Calculated Involvement (they stay involved as long as they like the deal).
What is rewarding gets done.	Intrinsic reasons.	Intrinsic Involvement (they stay involved without supervision).
What is thought to be good gets done.	Felt duties and obligations.	Moral Involvement (they stay involved without supervision and even when rewards are not available).

part of their personal and professional obligation to do what is best for children? Must change be something that comes primarily from the outside? Or can people be compelled to change by inner voices, and the moral voice of community? The argument in this chapter is that the meaning of change itself can be changed so that it becomes a natural part of the school. But for this kind of deinstitutionalization of change to occur, we must commit over the long haul to a different theory of schooling—an inside rather than an outside theory, a *gemeinschaft* theory rather than a *gesellschaft* theory, a theory that is more norms-based than rules-based.

Rules-based approaches to change rely on:

- Mandating new directions and practices, and then providing training and supervision to ensure their implementation
- Standardizing and tightly connecting the work that teachers do by engineering curriculum, teaching, scheduling, assessment, and other dimensions of the work flow in ways that script the behavior of teachers
- Standardizing the outcomes that teachers are to achieve in such detail that they all wind up doing pretty much the same things in order to get to the same place

All three approaches have appeal because they are simple to describe and understand. But all three approaches require complex management systems in order to be put into practice—systems that have unanticipated negative consequences for change. Structures must be in place. Roles must be identified and delineated. Expectations must be explicitly communicated. And monitoring systems must be established to ensure that planned changes are implemented properly. The more complex the management system that accompanies a change, the more likely is teacher discretion to be narrowed. And the more likely is teaching behavior simplified, routinized, and standardized. Teaching and learning suffers as a result. This condition then beckons new calls for reform. Rules-based options are searched again, and new change strategies are invented and implemented with the same effects. And so the cycle continues.

Exactly the opposite would be the case if rules-based approaches to change were replaced by such norms-based approaches as *pro-*

fessional socialization, purposing and shared values, and *collegiality and natural interdependence.* Norms-based approaches are conceptually more complex than rules-based approaches. But once they are understood, they do not require complex management systems for implementation in schools. This blessing, in turn, actually encourages teachers to practice in more complex ways. They are able to make decisions that are more responsive to the unique circumstances they face. And responsive decisions result in better teaching and learning conditions for students. Table 9.2 depicts these relationships.

Both competence and virtue are themes embedded in the concept of professional socialization. Competence refers to upgrading the knowledge base for teaching. Virtue emphasizes the professional obligations of a teacher. From a virtuous perspective, professionals are expected to commit themselves to a lifetime of inquiry, and to discipline themselves to practice at the edge of their crafts. Further, they are expected to be concerned not only with their own individual practice, but with the larger practice itself. And moreover, they are expected to make a moral commitment to help each other function successfully as members of this shared practice (Sergiovanni, 1992).

Increasing the capacity for teachers to practice competently and to behave virtuously will not be easy. But once both goals are achieved, professional socialization increases the likelihood that not only will teachers know what to do, when to do it, and how to do it, but that they will be committed to doing it well and without supervision. Relying on professional socialization as a change strategy may well be part of our future as more and more attention is given to upgrading the teaching profession. As we make progress on this front we will be able to worry a little less about how we are going to change things in schools. Change will become more of a way of life for teachers and less a planned occasion.

Purposing and shared values, it has been argued throughout this book, provide the glue that bonds people together in a loosely connected world. Both function as compass points and mileposts for guiding what is to be done and how, and both speak to us in the kind of moral voice that compels us to be responsive to change.

Collegiality and natural interdependence refer to the sharing of common work values and the way teachers help each other to

Table 9.2. Rules-Based and Norms-Based Change Strategies.

Change Strategy	Rules-Based			Norms-Based		
	Direct Supervision	Standardized Work	Standardized Outputs	Professional Socialization	Purposing and Shared Values	Collegiality and Inter-dependence
Strategy concept	Simple	Simple	Simple	Complex	Complex	Complex
Management system	Complex	Complex	Moderate	Simple	Simple	Simple
Teacher behavior	Simple	Simple	Moderate	Complex	Complex	Complex

get the job done properly. Both shared values and collegiality are sources of norms that emerge from within the school, that encourage people to become self-managing, and that guarantee that individuals and groups will make the changes needed for schools to work better.

With rules-based approaches, change usually has to be imposed somehow. With norms-based approaches, change typically gets taken care of naturally as part of daily life. In those few cases where it doesn't, deliberate planning for change happens close to where the action is, and involves the people who will count the most in its implementation.

In the Interim

Let's accept for a moment the premise that in the long run a *gemeinschaft* perspective on change will serve schools better than our present *gesellschaft* perspective. We will not be able to move from one to the other overnight. In the meantime, we must work in the environment we have now, not the one we want. Michael Fullan's ideas on educational change can help us develop the kinds of interim strategies that will move us closer to where we want to be. In his seminal work, *The New Meaning of Educational Change* (1991), he proposes certain do's and don'ts as basic to the successful implementation of educational change. They are worth paying attention to as we struggle to get from here to there:

1. Do not assume that your vision of what the change should be is the one that should or could be implemented. On the contrary, assume that one of the main purposes of the process of implementation is to exchange your reality of what should be through interaction with implementers and others concerned. Stated another way, assume that successful implementation consists of some transformation or continual development of initial ideas. (Particularly good discussions of the need for this assumption and the folly of ignoring it are contained in Lighthall, 1973; Marris, 1975, Chapter XVII; Schön, 1971, Chapter 5; Louis and Miles, 1990).
2. Assume that any significant innovation, if it is to result in change, requires individual implementers to work out their own meaning. Significant change involves a certain amount of ambiguity, ambivalence, and uncertainty for the individual

about the meaning of the change. Thus, effective implementation is a process of clarification. It is also important not to spend too much time in the early stages on needs assessment, program development, and problem definition activities—school staff have limited time. Clarification is likely to come in large part through practice (see Cohen, 1987; Loucks-Horsley and Hergert, 1985).

3. Assume that conflict and disagreement are not only inevitable but fundamental to successful change. Since any group of people possess multiple realities, any collective change attempt will necessarily involve conflict. Assumptions 2 and 3 combine to suggest that all successful efforts of significance, no matter how well planned, will experience an implementation dip in the early stages. Smooth implementation is often a sign that not much is really changing (Huberman and Miles, 1984).

4. Assume that people need pressure to change (even in directions that they desire), but it will be effective only under conditions that allow them to react, to form their own position, to interact with other implementers, to obtain technical assistance, etc. Unless people are going to be replaced with others who have different desired characteristics, relearning is at the heart of change.

5. Assume that effective change takes time. It is a process of "development in use." Unrealistic or undefined time lines fail to recognize that implementation occurs developmentally. Significant change in the form of implementing specific innovations can be expected to take a minimum of two or three years; bringing about institutional reforms can take five or more years. Persistence is a critical attribute of successful change.

6. Do not assume that the reason for lack of implementation is outright rejection of the values embodied in the change, or hard-core resistance to all change. Assume that there are a number of possible reasons: value rejection, inadequate resources to support implementation, insufficient time elapsed.

7. Do not expect all or even most people or groups to change. The complexity of change is such that it is impossible to bring about widespread reform in any large social system. Progress occurs when we take steps (e.g., by following the assumptions listed here) that increase the number of people affected. Our reach should exceed our grasp, but not by such a margin that we fall flat on our face. Instead of being discouraged by all that

remains to be done, be encouraged by what has been accomplished by way of improvement resulting from your actions.

8. Assume that you will need a plan that is based on the above assumptions and that addresses the factors known to affect implementation . . . Evolutionary planning and problem-coping models based on knowledge of the change process are essential (Louis and Miles, 1990).

9. Assume that no amount of knowledge will ever make it totally clear what action should be taken. Action decisions are a combination of valid knowledge, political considerations, on-the-spot decisions, and intuition. Better knowledge of the change process will improve the mix of resources on which we draw, but it will never and should never represent the sole basis for decisions.

10. Assume that changing the culture of institutions is the real agenda, not implementing single innovations. Put another way, when implementing particular innovations, we should always pay attention to whether the institution is developing or not.[1]

The tenth assumption, "Assume that changing the culture of institutions is the real agenda," is particularly key. In the end, changing schools is about changing cultures. This chapter has proposed that the likelihood for school cultures to be changed will be increased considerably if we are willing to adopt the norms-based perspective on change. Changing cultures is never easy. To understand change differently, we have to decide whether we will continue to struggle to invent new principles of change and new strategies for change that fit our present *gesellschaft* images of schools, or whether we will struggle to settle the issue once and for all by working to deinstitutionalize change.

Choosing to deinstitutionalize change requires providing teachers with contexts for sustained learning and for developing their profession. Do we really have a choice if we want to improve schools? McLaughlin and Talbert (1993) don't think so. Their research leads them to this conclusion: "Effecting and enabling the teacher learning required by systemic reform cannot be accomplished through

---

[1] Reprinted by permission of the publisher from Fullan, Michael, *The New Meaning of Educational Change* (2nd ed.). New York: Teachers College Press, 1991, pp. 105–107. (© 1991 by Teachers College, Columbia University. All rights reserved.)

traditional staff development models—episodic, decontextualized injections of "knowledge" and technique. The path to change in the classroom core lies within and through teachers' professional communities: learning communities which generate knowledge, craft new norms of practice, and sustain participants in their efforts to reflect, examine, experiment, and change" (p. 18).

Chapter Ten

The Politics of Virtue:
A New Compact

Margaret Mead once remarked, "Never doubt that a small group of thoughtful, committed citizens can change the world; indeed, it's the only thing that ever has." Her thought suggests that perhaps there is something to the thousand-points-of-light theory of change. I believe that it is possible to rally enough small groups of thoughtful and committed citizens throughout the continent to create the kind of schools we want if we are willing to change the way we think about leadership, and if we are willing to change the way we think about politics in schools.

Let's begin first with a comment about leadership. Chapter Five argued that schools need a leadership that enhances meaning, and a leadership that helps people solve the vexing problems schools face. Leadership for meaning is important because it provides the connections that enable parents, teachers, and students to know better who they are, and how they fit into a larger web of meaning and significance. Meaningful connections shore up the heart by providing moral direction, by enhancing commitment, and by instilling felt obligations that encourage everyone to do the right thing for the good of all. Without renewed connections, there is little prospect that efforts to restructure schools and to improve teaching and learning will succeed, no matter how well-conceived they might be. Leadership for problem solving is important because it provides the help school members need to understand the problems and issues they face, and the help they need to figure out what must be done to get them resolved. Meaning is needed to create community in schools. Problem solving is needed to make community work.

Leadership for meaning and leadership for problem solving were offered as contrasts to the corporate view of leadership that emphasizes leaders having visions, using these visions to create solutions, and then convincing followers to accept and implement these solutions. This is unworkable in today's schools. Instead, in Morrow's words:

> The sort of leader needed today is the kind who can assume a reasonably well-educated electorate, but help it sort through the inundations of information and opinion (much of it corrupt, self-serving, pseudo-moral) toward solutions. Americans need leaders who will not so much enforce a vision (though visions remain indispensable) as lead people to understand the problems they face together, and the costs and efforts necessary to solve them—the changes in behavior and attitudes sometimes, the sacrifices, and above all the need to think and adapt. The key to leadership now is to get Americans to act in concert, and take responsibility for the courses they have set for themselves [Morrow, 1994, p. 77].

The kind of leadership that Morrow envisions forces us to address the way we make decisions in schools. It calls for us to think anew what school politics is, and how it should work. Rarely does a day go by without the media telling us still another story of divisions, hostilities, factions, and other symptoms of disconnectedness. Teachers disagreeing over methods, parents bickering with teachers over discipline problems, board members squabbling over curriculum issues, administrators complaining about encroachments on their prerogatives, teachers and administrators differing on grading policies, everyone disagreeing on sex education, and students, feeling pretty much left out of it all, making it difficult for everyone in the school by tediously bartering their compliance and goodwill for things they want. This mixture of issues and this mixture of stakeholders, all competing for advantages, resembles a game where self-interest is the motivator, and where individual actors engage in the hard play of the *politics of division*. The purpose of this game is to win more for yourself than you have to give back in return. Graham Allison (1969) summarizes the game of politics of division as follows:

> Actions emerge neither as the calculated choice of a unified group nor as a formal summary of leader's preferences. Rather the con-

text of shared power but separate judgement concerning important choices determines that politics is the mechanism of choice. Note the *environment* in which the game is played: inordinate uncertainty about what must be done, the necessity that something be done and crucial consequences of whatever is done. These features force responsible men to become active players. *The pace of the game*— hundreds of issues, numerous games, and multiple channels— compels players to fight to "get others' attention," to make them "see the facts," to assure that they "take the time to think seriously about the broader issue." The *structure of the game*—power shared by individuals with separate responsibilities—validates each player's feeling that "others don't see my problem," and "others must be persuaded to look at the issue from a less parochial perspective." The *rules of the game*—he who hesitates loses his chance to play at that point, and he who is uncertain about his recommendation is overpowered by others who are sure—pressures players to come down on the side of a 51–49 issue and play. The *rewards of the game*—effectiveness, i.e., impact on outcomes, as the immediate measure of performance—encourages hard play [p. 710].

The predominance of the politics of division is a consequence of applying *gesellschaft* theories of governance, management, and organization to schools. Would things be different with *gemeinschaft* theories? Communities, too, "play the game" of politics. But it is a different game. It is a game of politics more like that envisioned by James Madison, Alexander Hamilton, John Jay, Thomas Jefferson, and other American Founders and enshrined in such sacred documents as "The Declaration of Independence," "The Constitution of the United States," and the amendments to that constitution that represent a bill of rights and a bill of responsibilities for all Americans. It is a game called *the politics of virtue*—a politics motivated by shared commitment to the common good and guided by protections that ensure the rights and responsibilities of individuals.

Three changes will be necessary in schools to substitute the politics of virtue for the politics of division:

- The bureaucratic and corporate values that have been borrowed from the *gesellschaft* world must be replaced with traditional democratic values that encourage a commitment to civic virtue.

- The rational choice theories of human nature that have been borrowed from the *gesellschaft* world must be replaced with a normative and moral theory of human nature.
- The executive images of leadership that have been borrowed from the *gesellschaft* world must be replaced with collegial images aimed at problem solving and ministering.

Civic Virtue

Chapter One stated that instead of importing our theories from business, we would be better off to renew our commitment to the democratic legacy that gave birth to the United States, and to use this legacy as the foundation for providing leadership to schools. The American Founders had in mind the creation of a covenantal polity within which "The body is one but has many members. There can be unity with diversity. . . . The great challenge was to create a political body that brought people together and created a 'we' but still enabled people to separate themselves and recognize and respect one another's individualities. This remains the great challenge for all modern democrats" (Elshtain, 1994, p. 9). The cultivation of commitment to civic virtue is a key part of this challenge.

During the debate over the constitution of 1787, America was faced with a choice between two conceptions of politics, republican and pluralist. In republican politics, civic virtue was considered to be the cornerstone principle—the prerequisite for the newly proposed government to work. Civic virtue was embodied in the willingness of citizens to subordinate their own private interests to the general good (see for example Sunstein, 1993), and was therefore the basis for creating a politics of virtue. This politics of virtue emphasized self-rule by the people, but not the imposition of their private preferences on the new government. Instead, preferences were to be developed and shaped by the people themselves for the benefit of the people as a polity.

Haefele (1993) believes that it is easier to provide examples of how civic virtue is expressed than to try to define it with precision. In his words:

> It is fashionable nowadays for both the left and the right to decry the loss of civic virtue; the left on such issues as industry rape of the

environment and the right because of the loss of patriotism. Both sides are undoubtedly right, as civic virtue belongs to no single party or creed. It is simply a quality of caring about public purposes and public destinations. Sometimes the public purpose is chosen over private purposes. A young Israeli economist investigating a Kibbutz came across the following case. The Kibbutz had money to spend. The alternatives were a TV antenna and TV sets for everyone or a community meeting hall. The economist found that everyone preferred the TV option but that, when they voted, they unanimously chose the meeting hall. Call it enlightened self-interest, a community preference or something else, it is civic virtue in action [p. 211].

When the republican conception of politics is applied to schools, *both* the unique shared values that define individual schools as covenantal communities, and our common democratic principles and conceptions of goodness that provide the basis for defining civic virtue are important.

The pluralist conception of politics differs markedly from the republican. Without the unifying power of civic virtue, factions strengthen and the politics of division reigns. In the ideal, the challenge of this politics is to play people and events in a way that the self-interests of individuals and factions are mediated in some orderly manner. "Under the pluralist conception, people come to the political process with pre-selected interests that they seek to promote through political conflict and compromise" (Sunstein, 1993, pp. 176). In Federalist paper No. 10, Alexander Hamilton (Hamilton, Madison, and Jay, [1787] 1961) proposed that deliberate governmental processes of conflict resolution and compromise, of checks and balances, be invented for this purpose. Checks and balances are needed because preferences are not shaped by the people themselves as they strive to control self-interest on behalf of the common good. Instead, preferences are imposed by the self-interests that happen to dominate at the time.

Civic virtue was important to both Federalists, who supported the proposed constitution, and Anti-Federalists, who opposed the constitution, though it was the centerpiece of Anti-Federalist thinking. The Anti-Federalists favored decentralization in the form of a direct democracy tempered by a commitment to the common good. The Federalists, by contrast, acknowledged the importance of civic virtue, but felt the pull of pluralistic politics was too strong for the embodiment of virtue to be left to chance. They proposed a representative rather than a direct form of government that would be guided by the principles of a formal constitution that specified a series of governmental checks and balances to control factionalism and self-interest.

The positions of both the Federalists and the Anti-Federalists have roles to play in the governance of schools. In small communities, for example, the politics of virtue expressed within a direct democracy guided by "citizen" devotion to the public good seems to make the most sense. Small schools and small schools within schools would be examples of such communities. They should be governed by autonomous school councils that are responsible for *both* educational policy and site-based management—both ends and means. This approach to governance represents a significant departure from present policies that allow principals, parents, and teachers in local schools to decide how they will do things, but not what they will do. The decisions that local school councils make should be guided by shared values and beliefs that parents, teachers, and students develop together. Schools, in this image, would not function as markets where self-interests reign or bureaucracies where entrenched rules systems reign, but as morally based direct democracies within which parents, teachers, and students, guided by civic virtue, make the best decisions possible for learning.

At the school district level, by contrast, the position of the Federalists might make the most sense. A representative form of government—spearheaded by elected school boards and guided by an explicit constitution containing the protections and freedoms needed to enable individual school communities to function autonomously—would be the model. School communities would have to abide by certain school district regulations regarding safety, due process, equity, fiscal procedures, and a few basic academic standards. But beyond these, schools would be free to decide for themselves their own educational purposes, their own educational programs, their own scheduling and ways of operating, and their own means to demonstrate to the school district and to the public that they are functioning responsibly.

The Rational Choice Question

It is a mistake to cast human beings into heroic images of sainthood as paragons of virtue. By definition, people are frail at best—prone to shortcuts, concerned about their own egos, and motivated by self-interest. But they also have the capacity to sacrifice their own self-interests for causes they believe in. And they also have the capacity to dream, to idealize, to pray, to wish for the best, to care for others, and to go beyond giving a fair day's work for a fair day's pay. Human nature is complex because it includes not only biological and psychological dimensions, but cultural ones as well.

By contrast, *gesellschaft* theories of human nature are anything but complex. Most can be traced back to a few principles that are at the center of classical economic theory. Prime among them is the "utility function," which is believed to explain all consumer behavior. The reasoning behind this belief is as follows: Humans are by their nature selfish. They are driven by a desire to maximize their self-interest and thus continually calculate the costs and benefits of their actions. They choose courses of action that either make them winners (they get a desired payoff) or keep them from losing (they avoid penalties). So dominant is this view and so pervasive is the concept of utility function that emotions such as love, loyalty, obligation, sense of duty, belief in goodness, commitment to a cause, and desire to help make things better are thought to count very little in determining the courses of actions that humans choose.

Another important economic principle is the belief that the individual counts the most. The individual is the prime decision maker who calculates costs and benefits of various alternatives and chooses courses of actions that are beneficial. The decisions of groups are acknowledged, but explained away as no more than the aggregate of many individual decisions. Both the concept of utility function and the idea that it is individuals and not groups that count comprise a model of economics called Rational Choice Theory.

Rational Choice Theory undergirds much of the thinking in schools about how to motivate teachers to perform, how to introduce school improvement initiatives in schools, how to motivate people to accept change, and how to motivate students to learn and to behave. Rational Choice Theory states: "What gets rewarded gets done." Chapter Nine discussed the consequences of overusing this rule. It noted that two other motivational rules are needed to provide a more complete picture of human nature: "What is rewarding gets done," and "What people value and believe in gets done." Both rules compel people to perform, to improve, to change, and to meet their commitments from within. Both rules address the intrinsic and moral nature of human nature.

Rational Choice Theory dominates our thinking and our practice. What are the consequences of this dominance? Haefele (1993) believes that Rational Choice Theory discourages the development of civic virtue. In his words:

> It is entirely possible that the greatest danger threatening American civic virtue was created by a sleight of hand in economic theory performed around the turn of the century. It was then that economists "solved" the vexed question of value by consigning it to the dust bin, replacing it with the concept of individual preference as the only source of values. By doing so, great advances were made in micro-theory as a self-contained, rational system. Once this system was fully developed, say with the publication of Paul Samuelson's *Foundations of Economic Analysis* (1947), economics re-emerged and began to define the rest of the social world in terms of rational choice models. That effort brought about a diminution of any and all ideas of civic virtue since all preferences . . . were considered equally valued, a disaster only now being addressed as economists work with philosophers, political theorists, and law professors [pp. 220–221].

Assigning all preferences equal value is a cardinal principle in the politics of division that now characterizes school policy and administration. All one needs to do is to identify the array of self-interest-motivated individual preferences and by doing a little addition, identify and settle on the preference that wins. "The squeaky wheel gets the oil." Any faction that screams loudly enough gets its way. By contrast, "Civic Virtue must, of course, address values and, in particular, public values—that is to say, shared values about public purposes and public destinations. If these are to be determined, willy-nilly, by the unconsidered preferences of the citizenry, then civic virtue is at best a sometime thing. While that ultimate rationalist . . . strives mightily to show that untrammeled individual preferences could result in a just society, it is clear to most that it could also result in total disaster" (Haefele, 1993, p. 221).

Is Civic Virtue for Students, Too?

Some readers might concede that we should move away from a rational choice view of motivation. We should acknowledge the capacity of parents and teachers to respond less in terms of their self-interest, and more in terms of what they believe is right and good. Readers might also concede that parents and teachers can engage in pursuits of the public good in a fashion that inspires them to higher levels of performance, and higher levels of ideals. But what about students? Can they too respond to the call of virtue?

Children and young adults in schools have different needs and different dispositions. They function developmentally at different levels of moral reasoning than do adults. But I think the evidence is overwhelming that students from kindergarten to grade 12 have the capacity to understand what civic virtue is and have the capacity to respond to it in ways that are consistent with their own levels of maturation.

For example, Rose Reissman (1993) and several other teachers in New York City's District 25 have been working with elementary school children (even first and second graders) on developing "bills of responsibilities." The bills are designed to teach the meaning of civic virtue, and to introduce students to sources of authority that are more morally based than the usual behavioristic ways to get students to do things. Key is the emphasis on reciprocal responsibilities—a critical ingredient in community building. Communities of mind, for example, evolve from commitments to standards that apply to everyone in the school, not just to students. Thus if students must be respectful, so must parents, teachers, principals, and everyone else who is a member of the school community, or who visits the school. Reissman describes what happened in one second grade classroom:

> First, the 2nd grade teacher asked her students to think about roles at home in which they "exercised responsibilities." The students identified roles such as child, foster child, daughter, son, sister, brother, granddaughter, pet owner, nephew, niece, and neighbor. (Many students lived in extended families or with unrelated adult guardians.) Using a standard format, the students listed or drew the responsibilities that were part of those roles.
>
> Among the role responsibility lists our 2nd graders generated were:

As a grandson, I am responsible to:

1. Help my grandma put on her clothes when her arthritis gets bad.
2. Pick up things from the floor for grandma.
3. Help grandma "see" dirt.
4. Remind grandma about her doctor's appointment.
5. Walk with grandma to her friends.
6. Fix up grandma's bureau top.

As the owner of Yips (my dog), I am responsible to:

1. Feed Yips three times a day.
2. Play with him when I get home.
3. Clean up after him if he has an accident.
4. Look to see where he is if I don't hear him.
5. Fill up and clean Yip's water dish and food plate.
6. Keep Yips away from Pendie the Parrot when she takes a bath.

Next, to study reciprocal relationships, the 2nd graders reviewed a contract their teacher had given them at the beginning of the year. The contract detailed the responsibilities of the teacher and the students. Among the teacher's responsibilities were helping the students learn, answering their questions, and making learning exciting. Students' responsibilities included arriving at school prepared to learn, having necessary supplies and textbooks, asking questions, and doing their homework.

To explore students' other reciprocal relationships, students interviewed family or community members whom they know. Among the relationships the students explored were: baby-sitter/child, parent/child, coffee shop owner/customer, grandparent/grandchild, and big brother/younger brother. They drafted Bills of Responsibility for those relationships, similar to the contract with their teacher.

Several parents wrote notes to the teachers telling them how much they enjoyed being interviewed by their children about their shared responsibilities [p. 86].

Two sixth grade classes at the East Port Orchard Elementary School in the state of Washington were asked recently, "If you could give a gift to East Port Orchard School that you couldn't buy or couldn't wrap, what would you give?" One class settled on love of learning, friendship, positive influence, help, tolerance of differences, honesty, caring, self-esteem. The other class settled on friendship, perseverance, love, recognition, trust, sense of belonging (East Port Orchard School, 1994).

The following example (Panasonic Foundation, 1994) describes civic virtue in action. A well-known sculptor had removed his limestone rhinoceros from its place in front of an art gallery in Bloomington, Indiana, to keep it from being vandalized. The K-12 students at the Harmony School launched a campaign to return the rhino to Bloomington. They raised $6,000 and purchased the rhino, which now stands in front of the school for the entire community to enjoy.

Last year, Harmony High School students decided that instead of the traditional field trip to Chicago, they would go to Quincy, Illinois, where the Mississippi floods had devastated the city. One of the students explained, "They have plenty of food, and plenty of relief supplies, but they don't have anybody to help get life in order." Harmony students helped by clearing mud, garbage, and debris from the streets, and by planting flowers and shrubs. Many similar stories, I know, are coming to your mind as you read about and think about the events at Harmony.

Harmony High School is private, and Bloomington, Indiana, is hardly downtown Kansas City, Miami, or San Antonio. But students everywhere are pretty much the same. They have the capacity to care. They want to be called to be good, and they know the difference between right and wrong. The fact is that students, too, under the right conditions, not only will be responsive to the calls of civic virtue, but they need to be responsive if they are to develop into the kinds of adults we want them to be.

Leadership for the Schoolhouse

"Do you know how many teachers we have in the class?" asked Elga [a kindergarten teacher] on the first day, a twinkle in her eye. Most of the students counted the adults in the room. One student guessed two, another three. "Would you like to meet all the teachers?" Elga asked. "Are you ready? You're going to be surprised! Watch me—I'm going to introduce them to you. My name is Elga

Brown. (She placed her hand on the shoulder of a child seated next to her) This is Steve. He's one of the teachers here. This is Jean. She's a teacher. I'll bet sometimes Jean's mom will be a teacher here." Elga continued around the circle introducing each person present. "We're all teachers here. Who do you think are the learners?" "All of us!" called out one excited boy (Meltzoff, 1994, pp. 16–17).

The essence of creating a politics of virtue for schools to replace *gesellschaft* politics is a redefined leadership. Leadership must be viewed as one important part of the web of moral obligations that administrators, teachers, parents, and even students must accept if they are to embody civic virtue. One part of this obligation is to share in the responsibility for exercising leadership. The other part of this obligation is to share in the responsibility for ensuring that leadership, whatever its source, is successful. In this redefinition, teachers continue to be responsible for providing leadership in classrooms. But students too have a moral obligation to help make things work. They too must provide leadership where they can, and they too must try as best they can to make the teacher's leadership effective. Similarly, administrators, parents, and teachers must accept responsibility together for the provision and the success of leadership.

Ronald Heifetz (1994) believes that leadership strategies should account for conditions and values that are consonant with the demands of our democratic society. "In addition to reality testing, these include respecting conflict, negotiation, and a diversity of views within a community; increasing community cohesion; developing norms of responsibility-taking, learning, and innovation; and keeping social distress within a bearable range" (p. 26).

Key to leadership in a democracy is the concept of social contract. Heifetz (1994) notes, "In part, democracy requires that average citizens become aware that they are indeed the principals, and that those upon whom they confer power are the agents. They have also to bear the risks, the costs, and the fruits of shared responsibility and civic participation" (p. 61).

The lessons are clear. Leadership for meaning, leadership for problem solving, collegial leadership, leadership as shared responsibility, leadership that serves school purposes, leadership that is tough enough to demand a great deal from everyone, and leadership that is tender enough to encourage the heart—these are the images of leadership we need for schools as communities.

Postscript:
Reconciling Individualism and Community

Gemeinschaft conceptions of schooling fit the developmental needs of students better, and are more likely to result in schools becoming more productive learning environments for students. This reality leads to the question of whether *gesellschaft* values are corrupt and should be replaced, or whether they have merit, but should not be applied to schools. One way to answer this question is by tackling it from a different perspective.

Oakeshott (1975, cited in Elkin, 1993), for example, makes a distinction between two kinds of associations in our society: enterprise and civil. Enterprise associations have formal goals. They require a layer of management whose job it is to decide the choice of means and to establish the structures needed to achieve these goals. Corporations are classical examples of enterprise associations. Civil associations, by contrast, do not have goals in a formal sense. They are, instead, settings within which members go about their self-determined pursuits guided by their subscription to norms of conduct that inform the decisions that they make. Families are classical examples of civil associations.

Enterprise associations derive their goals from external sources. Enterprise associations are then evaluated in terms of how well these goals are achieved. Civil associations, by contrast, develop their own goals as their members act out their self-determined priorities. They are evaluated in terms of how well individual and communal action reflects agreed-upon norms of conduct. Churches, for example, are not evaluated in terms of the number of souls saved, but in terms of whether they behave in holy ways.

Similarly, families are thought to be good if their behavior is good. Enterprise associations are *gesellschaft,* and civil associations are *gemeinschaft.*

My intent is not to call for the demise of enterprise associations. After all, in our technical-rational world, most of the associations in our society are closer to the enterprise end of the continuum than to the civil end. We should be thankful that this is the case. It would be hard to imagine effective armies, corporations, research institutions, hospitals, and libraries functioning without formal goals, clear lines of authority, competent and efficient management, and cost-effective accountability systems. But much as enterprise associations are prized in our society, so are civil associations.

Schools are not clear examples of either enterprise or civil associations. Nonetheless, most of us probably agree that they belong closer to the civil end of the continuum. The smaller schools get, the more they resemble families. Likewise, the more successful schools are in becoming the kinds of learning communities we want them to be, the more they should approach the civil-association end of the continuum.

For the most part, the literature of educational administration parallels the literature of business administration. The models that we use to think about issues, plan for change, prepare school leaders, and evaluate the effectiveness of schools were originally designed for use in enterprise associations. If schools are indeed more like civil associations than like enterprise associations, then we are using the wrong theories. And if this is the case, then we need to develop a new kind of leadership specifically for schools. I hope this book will help in that endeavor.

Let us accept the idea that schools are, first and foremost, civil associations and thus should be more family-like than corporation-like. Does this mean that schools should replace families? The answer is "No!" Families in all of their configurations must remain as the first and most important institution in the lives of our children. Schools should never be more than a second line of defense. As Amitai Etzioni (1993) explains:

> The best place to start is where each new generation acquires its moral anchoring: at home, in the family. We must insist once again

that bringing children into the world entails a moral responsibility to provide not only material necessities, but also moral education and character formation [p. 256].

Unfortunately, millions of American families have weakened to the point where their capacity to provide moral education is gravely impaired. And the fact is that communities have only a limited say over what families do. At best it will take years before a change in the moral climate restores parenting to its proper status and function for many Americans.

Thus, by default, schools now play a major role in character formation and moral education. Personal and communal responsibility come together here, for education requires the commitment of all citizens, not merely those who have children in school [p. 258].

Another issue is that of reconciling the two values of individualism and community. Many readers are probably asking, "Okay, so you argue compellingly for a renewed emphasis on communal understanding—on bringing people together to form webs of meaning around shared ideas that speak with a moral voice. But what about individual conscience? Isn't individualism an important value in our society, too? Wouldn't a more palatable and practical approach be to argue for striking a balance between the two by giving them *equal* attention?"

The "politically correct" response to these important questions is that both individual and community values are important. What we must do is give each equal attention by cutting the deck right down the middle. But I do not believe that this is the time to cut the cards in half. The answer is not to strike an equal balance. Instead we need a *correction* in our present course—a course that heavily favors individualism. Over the short term, at least, we need theories of schooling and theories of school leadership that give more attention to bringing people together, that give more attention to how we are alike than how we are different, and that give more attention to the cultivation of civic virtue. "Enough of the Pluribus, for the moment; a little more of the Unum" (Morrow, 1994, p. 77).

References

Allison, G. T. "Conceptual Models and the Cuban Missile Crisis." *The American Political Science Review,* 1969, *63*(3), 689–718.

Anderson, L. "Implementing Instructional Programs to Promote Meaningful, Self-Regulated Learning." In J. E. Brophy (ed.), *Advances in Research on Teaching,* Vol. 1 (pp. 311–343), Greenwich, Conn.: JAI, 1989.

Aristotle, *Nichomachean Ethics.* (D. Ross, trans.) New York: Oxford University Press, 1992.

Associated Press, "Most Students Cheat, Survey Says." *San Antonio Express News,* Oct. 20, 1993, p. 12–A.

Associated Press, "Dayton School Bans Lockers, Backpacks." *San Antonio Express News,* July 11, 1994, p. 9–A.

Barker, R. G., and Gump, P. V. *Big School, Small School.* Stanford, Calif.: Stanford University Press, 1964.

Barth, R. S. *Improving Schools from Within: Teachers, Parents, and Principals Can Make the Difference.* San Francisco: Jossey-Bass, 1990.

Bass, B. M., *Leadership and Performance Beyond Expectations.* New York: Free Press, 1985.

Bellah, R. N., and others. *Habits of the Heart: Individualism and Commitment in American Life.* New York: HarperCollins, 1985.

Benson, P. L., and Guerra, M. J. *Sharing the Faith: The Beliefs and Values of Catholic High School Teachers.* Washington, D.C.: National Catholic Educational Association, 1985.

Bimber, B. *The De-Centralization Mirage: Comparing Decision-Making Arrangements in Four High Schools.* Santa Monica, Calif.: Rand, 1994.

Bolin, F. S. "Reassessment and Renewal in Teaching." In F. S. Bolin and J. M. Falk (eds.). *Teacher Renewal: Professional Issues, Personal Choices.* New York: Teachers College Press, 1987.

Bonstingl, J. J. *Schools of Quality: An Introduction to Total Quality Management in Education.* Alexandria, Va.: Association for Supervision and Curriculum Development, 1992.

Boyer, E. "The Basic School: Focusing on the Child." *Principal,* 1994, *73*(3), 19–32.

Bradley, A. "By Asking Teachers About 'Context' of Work, Center Moves to the Cutting Edge of Research." *Education Week*, March 31, 1993.

Brandt, R. "On Making Sense: A Conversation with Magdalene Lampert." *Educational Leadership*, 1994, *51*(5), 26–30.

Brophy, J. E. "Probing the Subtle Ties of Subject-Matter Teaching." *Educational Leadership*, 1992, *49*(7), 4–8.

Brown, A. "The Advancement of Learning." *Educational Research*, 1994, *23*(8), 4–12.

Bruner, J. S., and Postman, L. "On the Perception of Incongruity: A Paradigm." *Journal of Personality*, 1949, *18*(1), 206–223.

Bryk, A. S., and Driscoll, M. E. *The High School as Community: Contextual Influences and Consequences for Students and Teachers*. Madison: Wisconsin Center for Education Research, 1988.

Burns, J. M. *Leadership*. New York: HarperCollins, 1978.

Cartwright, M. Presentation to the Principals' Center, Trinity University, San Antonio, Tex., Oct. 21, 1993.

Cawelti, G. "High School Restructuring: A National Study," Arlington, Va.: Educational Research Services, 1994.

Clark, D. L., and Meloy, J. "Renouncing Bureaucracy: A Democratic Structure For Leadership in Schools." In T. J. Sergiovanni and J. H. Moore (eds.), *Schooling For Tomorrow: Directing Reforms to Issues That Count*. Needham Heights, Mass.: Allyn & Bacon, 1989.

Cohen, M. "Designing State Assessment Systems." *Phi Delta Kappan*, 1987, *7*(8), 583–588.

Combs, A. "Personality Theory and Its Implications for Curriculum Development." In A. Frazier (ed.), *Learning More About Learning*. Washington, D.C.: National Education Association for Supervision and Curriculum Development, 1959.

Conant, J. *The American High School Today: A First Report to Interested Students*. New York: McGraw Hill, 1959.

Convey, J. J. "Catholic Schools and Community." *NCEA Notes [National Catholic Education Association]*, 1991, *24*(1).

Deal, T. E., and Kennedy, A. A. *Corporate Cultures*. Reading, Mass.: Addison-Wesley, 1982.

Deci, E. L., and Ryan, R. M. *Intrinsic Motivation and Self-Determinism in Human Behavior*. New York: Plenum, 1985.

De Pree, M. *Leadership Is an Art*. New York: Doubleday, 1989.

Dorn, R. "The Changing Roles of Principals and Staff Members." *Wingspan*, 1995, *10*(2), 7–10.

East Port Orchard School, "Community Forum." East Port Orchard, Wash., Dec. 7, 1994.

Edwards, C. "Partner, Nurturer, and Guide: The Role of the Reggio Teacher in Action." In C. Edwards, L. Gandini, and G. Forman, *The Hundred*

Languages of Children: The Reggio Emilia Approach to Early Childhood Education. Norwood, N.J.: Ablex, 1993.

Elkin, S. L. "Constitutionalism: Old and New." In S. L. Elkin and K. E. Soltan (eds.), *A New Constitutionalism.* Chicago: University of Chicago Press, 1993.

Elshtain, J. B. "Democracy and the Politics of Difference." *The Responsive Community,* 1994, *4*(2), 9–20.

Etzioni, A. *The Moral Dimension: Toward a New Economics.* New York: Free Press, 1988.

Etzioni, A. *The Spirit of Community: Rights, Responsibilities, and the Communitarian Agenda.* New York: Crown, 1993.

Evans, M. "The Model in Ministry." Dissertation in progress, United Theological Seminary, Dayton, Ohio, 1994.

Feinberg, W. *Japan and the Pursuit of a New American Identity.* New York: Routledge & Kegan Paul, 1993.

Fillipinni, T. "Introduction to the Reggio Approach." Symposium presentation. National Association for the Education of Young Children. Washington, D.C., Nov. 16, 1990.

Fiske, E. B. "Lessons: Are Private Schools Better Because They Have Fewer Administrators?" *The New York Times,* Aug. 31, 1988.

Fowler, W. J., Jr. "School Size, School Characteristics, and School Outcomes." Paper presented at the annual meeting of the American Educational Research Association, San Francisco, 1989.

Fox, K. "Educator Testifies Teen Killer Bowed to Peer Pressure." *Express News,* July 20, 1994, p. 1–C.

Fullan, M. G. *The New Meaning of Educational Change.* New York: Teachers College Press, 1991.

Fullan, M. G. "Coordinating Top-Down and Bottom-Up Strategies for Educational Reform." In R. F. Elmore and S. H. Furhrman, (eds.), *The Governance of Curriculum.* The 1994 Yearbook of the Association for Supervision and Curriculum Development. Alexandria, Va., 1994.

Gardner, H. *Frames of Mind: The Theory of Multiple Intelligences.* New York: Basic Books, 1983.

Gardner, H. "Re-Introducing *Frames of Mind.*" Introduction to the Paperback Edition of *Frames of Mind,* New York: Basic Books, 1985.

Gardner, H. "Balancing Specialized and Comprehensive Knowledge: The Growing Educational Challenge." In T. J. Sergiovanni and J. H. Moore (eds.), *Schooling for Tomorrow: Directing Reforms to Issues That Count.* Needham Heights, Mass.: Allyn & Bacon, 1989.

Gardner, J. W. "The Heart of the Matter: Leader-Constituent Interaction." *Leadership Papers No. 3.* Washington D.C.: Independent Sector, June 1986a.

Gardner, J. W. "The Tasks of Leadership." *Leadership Papers No. 2.* Washington, D.C.: Independent Sector, March 1986b.

Gerstner, L. V., Jr., Semerad, R. D., Doyle, D. P., and Johnston, W. B. *Reinventing Education Entrepreneurship in America's Public Schools.* New York: Dutton, 1994.

Gleick, J. *Chaos: Making a New Science.* New York: Viking Penguin, 1987.

Goodlad, J. *A Place Called School: Prospects for the Future.* New York: McGraw-Hill, 1984.

Greene, D., and Lepper, M. R. "How to Turn Play Into Work." *Psychology Today,* 1974, *8*(4), pp. 49–52.

Gregory, T. "Small Is Too Big: Achieving a Critical Anti-Mass in the High School." A position paper prepared for the Hubert H. Humphrey Institute for Public Affairs and the North Central Regional Educational Laboratory, Sept. 1992, Minneapolis, Minn.

Gregory, T., and Smith, G. R. *High Schools as Communities: The Small School Reconsidered.* Bloomington, Ind.: Phi Delta Kappa Foundation, 1987.

Haefele, E. T. "What Constitutes the American Republic?" In S. L. Elkin and K. E. Soltan (eds.), *A New Constitutionalism.* Chicago: University of Chicago Press, 1993.

Hamilton, A., Madison, J., and Jay, J. "The Federalist Papers." (C. Rossitern, ed.) New York: New American Library, 1961. (The eighty-five papers in the collection were originally published between 1787 and 1788.)

Hargrove, E. C. "Two Conceptions of Institutional Leadership." In B. D. Jones (ed.), *Leadership and Politics: New Perspectives in Political Science.* Lawrence: University of Kansas Press, 1989.

Hayes, R. H. "Strategic Planning—Forward in Reverse?" *Harvard Business Review,* Nov.-Dec. 1985, 111–119.

Heath, D. H. *Schools of Hope: Developing Mind and Character in Today's Youth.* San Francisco: Jossey-Bass, 1994.

Heifetz, R. *Leadership: No Easy Answers.* Cambridge, Mass.: Belknap Press, 1994.

Hertzberg, F. *Work and the Nature of Man.* New York: World, 1966.

Hill, P. T., Foster, G. E., and Gendler, T. *High Schools with Character.* Santa Monica, Calif.: Rand, 1990.

Holt, M. "Dr. Deming and the Improvement of Schooling: No Instant Pudding." *Journal of Curriculum and Supervision,* 1993, *10*(1), 6–23.

Huberman, A., and Miles, D. *Innovation Up Close.* New York: Plenum, 1984.

Jenks, C. *The New York Times.* Dec. 12, 1965.

Johnson, S. *Teachers at Work: Achieving Success in Schools.* New York: Basic Books, 1990.

Kaplan, A. *The Conduct of Inquiry: Methodology for Behavioral Science.* San Francisco: Chandler, 1964.

Katz, L. "What Can We Learn from Reggio Emilia?" In C. Edwards, L. Gandini, and G. Forman, *The Hundred Languages of Children: The Reggio Emilia Approach to Early Childhood Education.* Norwood, N.J.: Ablex, 1993.

Kearns, D. J. "A Business Perspective on American Schooling." *Education Week,* Apr. 20, 1988.

Kelly, R. E. "In Praise of Followers." *Harvard Business Review.* Nov./Dec. 1988, pp. 142–148.

Kleinfeld, J. "No Shortage of Characters in the North." *Fairbanks Daily News-Miner,* Apr. 14, 1993.

Kohn, A. *No Contest: The Case Against Competition.* Boston: Houghton-Mifflin, 1986.

Kornhaber, M., and Gardner, H. *Varieties of Excellence: Identifying and Assessing Children's Talents.* Teacher's College, Columbia University National Center for Restructuring Education, Schools and Teaching, 1993.

Kuhn, T. S. "The Structure of Scientific Revolutions." *The International Encyclopedia of Unified Science* (2nd ed.), 2 vols. Chicago: University of Chicago Press, 1970.

Lemming, J. S. "Character Education and the Creation of Community." *The Responsive Community,* 1994, *4*(4), 49–57.

Lewis, H. *A Question of Values.* New York: HarperCollins, 1990.

Lichtenstein, G., McLaughlin, M., and Knudsen, J. "Teacher Empowerment and Professional Knowledge." In A. Lieberman (ed.), *The Changing Context of Teaching.* Ninety-First Yearbook of the National Society for the Study of Education. Chicago: University of Chicago Press, 1992.

Lickona, T. "The Return of Character Education." *Educational Leadership,* 1993, *51*(3), 6–11.

Lieberman, A., and Miller, L. *Teachers, Their World, and Their Work.* Alexandria, Va.: Association for Supervision and Curriculum Development, 1984.

Lieberman, A., and Miller, L. "School Improvement: Themes and Variations." In A. Lieberman (ed.), *Rethinking School Improvement: Research Craft and Concept.* New York: Teachers College Press, 1986.

Lighthall, F. "Multiple Realities and Organizational Nonsolutions: An Essay on Anatomy of Educational Innovation." *School Review,* 1973, *81*(2), pp. 255–293.

Lipsky, M. *Street-Level Bureaucracy: Dilemmas of the Individual in Public Services.* New York: Basic Books, 1980.

Little, J. W. "Teachers Professional Development in a Climate of Educational

Reform." *Educational Evaluational Policy Analysis,* Summer 1993, *15*(2), 129–152.

Lortie, D.C. *School Teacher: A Sociological Study.* Chicago: University of Chicago Press, 1975.

Loucks-Horsley, S., and Hergert, L. *An Action Guide to School Improvement.* Arlington, Va.: Association for Supervision and Curriculum Development and The Network, 1985.

Louis, K., and Miles, M. D. *Improving the Urban High School· What Works and Why.* New York: Teachers College Press, 1990.

Macdonald, J. B. "An Image of Man: The Learner Himself." In R. C. Doll (ed.), *Individualized Instruction.* Washington, D.C.: National Education Association for Supervision and Curriculum Development, 1964.

MacIntyre, A. *After Virtue: A Study in Moral Theory.* Notre Dame, Ind.: University of Notre Dame Press, 1981.

Mannheim, K. *Man and Society in an Age of Reconstruction.* New York: Harcourt Brace & Company, 1940.

March, J. G., and Simon, H. A. *Organizations.* New York: John Wiley, 1958.

Marris, P. *Loss and Change.* New York: Anchor Press/Doubleday, 1975.

Martinez, R. "New School Year Brings Change." *San Antonio Express News,* Aug. 14, 1994, p. 5–B.

McDonnell, L., and Elmore, R. "Getting the Job Done: Alternative Policy Instruments." *Educational Evaluation and Policy Analysis,* 1987, *9*(2), 133–152.

McLaughlin, M., and Talbert, J. E. *Contexts That Matter for Teaching and Learning.* Stanford, Calif.: Stanford University, Center for Research as the Context of Secondary School Teaching, 1993.

Meier, D. "The Kindergarten Tradition in High School." In K. Jarvis and C. Montag (eds.), *Progressive Education for the 1990s: Transforming Practice.* New York: Teachers College Press, 1991.

Meier, D. "Reinventing Teaching." *Teachers College Record,* 1992, *93*(4), 594–609.

Meltzoff, N. "Relationship, The Fourth 'R': The Development of a Classroom Community." *The School Community Journal,* 1994, *4*(2), 13–26.

Minneapolis Public Schools, "News Release, July 19, 1994." *Panasonic Partnership Program, a newsletter of the Panasonic Foundation,* 1994, *3*(2).

Mintzberg, H. "If You're Not Serving Bill and Barbara, Then You're Not Serving Leadership." In J. G. Hunt, U. Sekaran, and C. Schriesheim (eds.), *Leadership Beyond Establishment Views.* Carbondale: Southern Illinois University, 1982.

Morris, V. C., Crowson, R. L., Porter-Gehrie, C., and Hurwitz, E. *Principals in Action: The Reality of Managing Schools.* Columbus, Ohio: Merrill, 1984.

Morrow, L. "The Real Points of Light." *Time*, Dec. 5, 1994, pp. 76–77.

Morse, R. A. Research Review: "Honey Bees Have Solved the Problem of Finding and Exploiting the Best Food Source Available. Exciting News For Bee Keepers, Business Schools, and Psychologists." *Gleanings in Bee Culture*, Jan. 1992.

Murgatroyd, S., and Morgan, C. *Total Quality Management in School.* Philadelphia: Hoppen University Press, 1993.

Nanus, B. *Visionary Leadership: Creating a Compelling Sense of Direction for Your Organization.* San Francisco: Jossey-Bass, 1992.

Nathan, J. *Free to Teach: Achieving Equity and Excellence in Schools.* Minneapolis, Minn.: Winston Press, 1983.

New York Times Service. "Small Schools, Not Racial Make-up Help Boost Academic Performance." *San Antonio Express News*, Sep. 25, 1994.

Noddings, N. *The Challenge to Care in Schools.* New York: Teachers College Press, 1992.

Nuxoll, C. "A Response to Dr. Thomas Sergiovanni's Themes." Washington State Association for Supervision and Curriculum Development Conference, Critical Issues Institute Symposium, Spokane, Wash., Feb. 3, 1994.

Oakeshott, M. *On Human Conduct.* Oxford, England: Clarendon Press, 1975.

O'Neil, J. "Change Starts with the Individual, Fullan Contends." *ASCD Update*, May 1994, *36*(4).

Panasonic Foundation. "Panasonic Partnership Program." *Panasonic Partnership Program, a newsletter of the Panasonic Foundation,* 1994, *4*(1).

Parker, M. J. "Teaching Virtues Favored by Many." *San Antonio Express News*, Aug. 13, 1994, p. 14.

Parsons, T. *The Social System.* New York: Free Press, 1951.

Perkins, D., and Blythe, T. "Putting Understanding Up Front." *Educational Leadership*, 1994, *51*(5), 4–7.

Perrone, V. "Supporting Teacher Growth." *Childhood Education*, 1978, *54*(6), 298–302.

Peters, T. "Business Can Learn from Military Strategy." *San Antonio Light*, Jan. 24, 1989a.

Peters, T. "Structure Vs. Spirit Battle Lines Are Drawn." *San Antonio Light*, July 25, 1989b.

Peters, T. J., and Waterman, R. H. *In Search of Excellence.* New York: HarperCollins, 1982.

Plato. *The Republic of Plato.* (F. M. Cornford, trans.) Oxford, England: Clarendon Press, 1941.

Pohly, K. *Transforming the Rough Places: The Ministry of Supervision.* Dayton, Ohio: Whaleprints, 1993.

Prawat, R. "Promoting Access to Knowledge, Strategy, and Disposition in

Students: A Research Synthesis." *Review of Educational Research*, 1989, *59*, 1–41.

Prawat, R. S. "From Individual Differences to Learning Communities— Our Changing Focus." *Educational Leadership*, 1992, *49*(7), 9–13.

Prawat, R. S. "The Role of the Principal in the Development of Learning Communities." *Wingspan: The Pedamorphosis Communique*, 1993, *9*(2), 7–9.

Reissman, R. "A Bill of Responsibilities." *Educational Leadership*, 1993, *51*(4), 86–87.

Resnick, L. "Literacy in School and Out." *Daedalus*, 1990, *119*(2), 169–185.

Rivera, M. "Neighborhood Schools: One Short Route To Reform." *Education Week*, 1994, *13*(18), 39–40.

Salinger, J.D. *The Catcher in the Rye.* Boston: Little, Brown, 1951.

Samuelson, P. *Foundations of Economic Analysis.* Cambridge, Mass.: Harvard University Press, 1947.

San Antonio Express News. "Growing Up in the Garden." Apr. 30, 1994, p. 18–A.

Saphier, J., and D'Auria, J. *How to Bring Vision to School Improvement Through Core Outcomes, Commitments, and Beliefs.* Carlisle, Mass.: Research for Better Teaching, Inc., 1993.

Sarason, S. *The Predictable Failure of Educational Reform: Can We Change Course Before It's Too Late?* San Francisco: Jossey-Bass, 1990.

Schaefer, R. J. *The School as a Center of Inquiry.* New York: HarperCollins, 1967.

Scherer, M. "On Schools Where Students Want to Be: A Conversation with D. Meier." *Educational Leadership*, Sep. 1994, *52*(1), 4–8.

Schön, D. *Beyond the Stable State.* New York: Norton, 1971.

Selznick, P. *Leadership in Administration.* Berkeley: University of California Press, 1957.

Senge, P. M. *The Fifth Discipline: The Art and Practice of the Learning Organization.* New York: Doubleday, 1990.

Sergiovanni, T. J. *The Principalship: A Reflective Practice Perspective.* Needham Heights, Mass.: Allyn & Bacon, 1987a.

Sergiovanni, T. J. "Will We Ever Have a True Profession?" *Educational Leadership*, 1987b, *44*(8), 44–49.

Sergiovanni, T. J. "Developing a Practical Theory of Educational Administration." Address to the Educational Management Congress, Rand Afrikaans University, Johannesburg, Republic of South Africa, Sept. 14, 1989.

Sergiovanni, T. J. *Value-Added Leaderships.* San Diego: Harcourt Brace Jovanovich College Division, 1990.

Sergiovanni, T. J. *The Principalship: A Reflective Practice Perspective.* (2nd ed.) Needham Heights, Mass.: Allyn & Bacon, 1991.

Sergiovanni, T. J. *Moral Leadership: Getting to the Heart of School Improvement.* San Francisco: Jossey-Bass, 1992.

Sergiovanni, T. J. *Building Community in Schools.* San Francisco: Jossey-Bass, 1994.

Sergiovanni, T. J. *The Principalship: A Reflective Practice Perspective.* (3rd ed.) Needham Heights, Mass.: Allyn & Bacon, 1995.

Sergiovanni, T. J., and Elliot, D. L. *Educational and Organizational Leadership in Elementary Schools.* Englewood Cliffs, N.J.: Prentice Hall, 1975.

Shives, J. A. "Review of A. S. Bryk, V. E. Lee, and P. B. Holland, *Catholic Schools and the Common Good.*" Cambridge, Mass.: Harvard University Press, 1993. In *Harvard Educational Review,* 1994, *64*(3), 339–344.

Shulman, L. S. "Teaching Alone, Teaching Together: Needed Agendas for the New Reforms." In T. J. Sergiovanni and J. H. Moore (eds.), *Schooling for Tomorrow: Directing Reforms to Issues That Count.* Needham Heights, Mass.: Allyn & Bacon, 1989.

Shuster, B. "CLAS Tests Anger Students Even as They Spur Thought." *Los Angeles Times,* May 23, 1994, p. 1–B.

Sirotnik, K. A. "The School as the Center of Change." In T. J. Sergiovanni and J. H. Moore (eds.), *Schooling for Tomorrow: Directing Reforms to Issues That Count.* Needham Heights, Mass.: Allyn & Bacon, 1989.

Smith, R. M. "American Conceptions of Citizenship and National Service." *The Responsive Community,* 1993, *3*(3), 14–27.

Snyder, K. J. "Welcome to the Quality Revolution." *Wingspan: The Pedamorphosis Communique,* 1994, *10*(1), 2–3.

Staw, B. "Leadership and Persistence." In T. J. Sergiovanni and J. E. Corbally (eds.), *Leadership and Organizational Culture.* Urbana: University of Illinois Press, 1984.

Sunstein, C. R. "The Enduring Legacy of Republicanism." In S. L. Elkin and K. E. Soltan (eds.), *A New Constitutionalism.* Chicago: University of Chicago Press, 1993.

Tannenbaum, A. *Control in Organizations.* New York: McGraw Hill, 1968.

Terry, R. W. *Authentic Leadership: Courage in Action.* San Francisco: Jossey-Bass, 1993.

Texas Education Agency, "Learner-Centered Schools For Texas: Vision of Texas Educators." State-adopted proficiencies for Texas, 1994.

Tonnies, F. *Gemeinschaft und Gesellschaft.* [Community and Society]. (C. P. Loomis, ed. and trans.), New York: HarperCollins, 1957. (Originally published 1887.)

United Theological Seminary. *United Theological Seminary Doctor of Ministry Handbook,* Dayton, Ohio, 1994.

U.S. Department of Labor. *What Work Requires of Schools: A SCANS Report for America 2000.* Washington, D.C., 1991.

van Manen, M. *The Tact of Teaching: The Meaning of Pedagogical Thoughtfulness.* Albany: State University of New York Press, 1991.

Viadero, D. "Ideas and Findings." *Education Week,* 1994a, *8*(35), 34.

Viadero, D. "Ideas and Findings." *Education Week,* 1994b, *8*(39), 38.

Walberg, H. J., and Walberg, H. J., III. "Losing Local Control." *Educational Researcher,* 1994, *23*(5), 19–26.

Webster, N. "The Big Picture For Little People." *Education Week.* 1994, *8*(40), p. 52.

Weick, K. "Educational Organizations as Loosely Coupled Systems." *Administrative Science Quarterly,* 1976, *21*(2), 1–19.

Weick, K. "The Concept of Loose Coupling: An Assessment." *Organizational Theory Dialogue,* Dec. 1986.

Whitehead, B. "The Failure of Sex Education." *The Atlantic Monthly,* 1994, *274*(4), pp. 55–81.

Yatvin, J. "Catchers in the Rye." *Education Week,* 1994, *14*(2), p. 37.

Yeager, R. J., Benson, P. L., Guerra, M. J., and Manno, B. V. *The Catholic High School: A National Portrait.* Washington, D.C.: Catholic Educational Association, 1985.

Index